FLOWERS
in the Modern Manner

FLOWERS
in the
Modern
Manner

Marian Aaronson

GB

Grower Books : London

Acknowledgements

I would like to thank Ken Lauder for the
excellent photographs, David Weaver
for the meticulous line drawings,
Jonathan Sharp the book designer and the
many flower arranging friends at home
and abroad who encouraged me to
attempt a third book.

Grower Books
50 Doughty Street
London WC1N 2LP

First published 1981
Reprinted 1984

© Grower Books 1981

ISBN Cased: 0 901361 53 4
       Paperback: 0 901361 54 2

Designed and produced by Sharp Print Management
Printed in Great Britain

To Jack, who puts up with
being a flower arranger's husband.

Contents

About the Author

Marian Aaronson, who comes from
Wales, started flower arranging some
twenty years ago. Since then she has
become internationally known and has
travelled extensively overseas. She makes
regular visits to many continental flower
clubs, to teach and lecture, and has
judged at many International flower
shows. Here at home, too, she is much in
demand as an instructor in the modern
style of flower arranging.

About the book

What does the word modern really mean, and how does it apply to the art of flower arranging? The various terms used to define different styles of artistic expression are often ambiguous because it is not really easy to make clear-cut divisions between each category, or to give entirely straightforward definitions.

When we refer to traditional flower arranging, it is to a style that has become familiar and acceptable through long association and usage. Broadly, this indicates those arrangements put together in a conventional manner following established principles and theories.

The word modern suggests something new, and up-dating, present thinking, and a break with the past. A modern flower arrangement mirrors to-day's ideas and artistic attitudes, and has become identified with the sparser, sophisticated design that stretches beyond the conventional. The arranger in this instance has broken away from tradition to experiment in a wider area of designing. This gives greater flexibility to be original and innovative in presenting ideas since there is more freedom for self-expression.

The ultra-modern design is indeed dramatically different in form and concept to the conventional flower arrangement and reflects the influence of other modern art forms. In the abstract style, plant material is used in a non-naturalistic manner, and its elusive, rather than more obvious aspects considered, and presented in a simplified form according to personal impressions.

Today's flower arrangements are, in general, very design orientated, and this is extended, not only to the streamlined modern arrangement, but to many variations and categories of style. For, after all, trends have evolved gradually, and old and new aspects often intermingle and modify one another, and the principles and theories of one style can be adapted to or can influence the approach to another. Traditional designs are often 'modernised'. Today's mass arrangement for instance, is far less packed, so that the individual plant material is more easily identifiable than in the mass of old. There is a crisper outline incorporating the element of space, which gives a looser and more graceful silhouette. Landscape and interpretative designs are on the whole, more controlled and under-stated, with maximum effect often achieved with the minimum of plant material and accessories.

On the other hand, there are conventional aspects often incorporated in some modern designs, where the line is crisp and clear cut, but the plant material still assembled in a traditional manner, and a more conventional pattern.

The modern way of 'doing the flowers' therefore is a new experience based on traditional principles, as a firm foundation on which to build new images. Knowledge of the basic art principles is still the strongest beam in the designing structure, and experience gives the confidence to be more ingenious and inventive. Modern design does not rely on a large quantity of material for effect, but on the imaginative use of a little. It challenges the designer to use whatever is available in new and attractive ways. Many modern arrangements are flowerless, with other interesting forms of plant life used with panache. Distinctive contrasts of colour, shape and texture often replaces masses of material, and it is the ingenuity displayed in putting everything together that gives distinction and the arrangement its character and charisma.

It is this aspect of flower arranging that interests me most and this book will perhaps encourage you also to take advantage of the continuing challenge and artistic individuality that modern flower arranging offers, so that we need not become over-dependent on the practised style but can constantly evolve to a greater challenge.

The analysis of each arrangement with picture and words might explain what motivates me, and the way I work, which could be a stimulus to your own ideas and imagination.

The variety of style and presentation illustrates how the concepts apply in different forms of design rather than as confined to one specific area. By breaking down the designing procedure, illustrated with detailed line drawings and design analysis, it is easier to grasp the aims of each composition and how specific effects are achieved.

The explanation of the technical aspects, as applied to each arrangement might encourage you to try the more difficult and original presentations. Besides, it is a comfort to know that overcoming the mechanical obstacles is often the toughest hurdle, and that this is difficult for everyone, however splendid the personal vision or the creative talent.

You will naturally invent the technique and form of expression most compatible to your temperament and requirements, and you will not necessarily base these on my approach. I would however like to think that my enthusiasm and explanations will confirm the value of cultivating an individual style so that each arrangement is a reflection of *your* enthusiasm and personality.

About Design

Design is really rather a dull word that is more likely to suggest the practical and the prosaic rather than the poetic. Yet a fine design, that is visually pleasing is based not only on structural correctness and technical efficiency, but governed also by sensitivity to the laws of balance, harmony, and rhythm and an appreciation of what is orderly and unified. A design born of inspiration is more than just mathematical perfection.

Kenneth F. Bates in his book on *Basic Design* maintains that a 'good design is one to which no more can be added and at the same time one from which nothing can be subtracted without causing an emptiness or feeling of incompletion'. There is much in this statement that is wise and profound and its philosophy can be of great value in assessing our own or another's work.

It implies a simplicity of purpose to achieve an orderly composition that speaks to the viewer in a clear and uncomplicated manner without the confusion of unnecessary detail. The process involves balancing shape with space, organising colour and texture for maximum effect and tying together the different units in a rhythmical manner to create a feeling of wholeness and completeness. In a good design there is harmony and affinity between the units to create a comfortable sense of each belonging to and working for each other, and the total enhancement. There are areas that stimulate interest and excitement, contrasted by areas of rest for quiet contemplation and refreshment for the eye and mind. There is sufficient variety to avoid boredom, but nothing superfluous spoils design simplicity, either in the amount of plant material and accessories used, the ideas expressed, or the techniques adopted.

Clearly, discipline and restraint help to preserve the purity of the design whatever its concept. It is easier to be analytical and take positive action when being objective (which explains why it is easier to spot other people's mistakes). When in doubt or striving for improvement it is helpful to ask the following questions.

1. Is the selection of material and everything used suitable and harmonious to the nature and purpose of the design envisaged? Can this be improved upon?
2. Have the units been organised in a way that is sympathetic to the needs of the design? Study line, and function of space, use of advancing and receding elements, and the overall balance.
3. Is anything superfluous? Be ruthless, query the function of each unit and its design contribution.
4. What is missing? Not enough contrast? Can presentation be improved, by raising the arrangement, or altering the angle at which it is viewed? Would background help?
5. Does the finished composition appear unified? Are the proportions and the balance pleasing? Does any area dominate at the expense of the overall interest of the design?
6. When working to a theme, is there an effective expressive element? Is the title well interpreted? Does it communicate the message?

These are general guidelines only, as every situation is unique and involves different design requirements, otherwise designing would be extremely monotonous. Every arrangement is coloured by individual temperament and outlook, and time and place and the purpose. Nevertheless, although the laws are flexible to different demands and there are infinite variations in presentation, the fundamentals of design remain constant and the principles unchanging. A growing interest and greater experience will give greater confidence to test new methods and search for ever more variations of a basic pattern.

Developing a taste for design and keeping the interest level high, should not be difficult for flower arrangers. As designers with plant material, we have the added advantage of a medium that is itself inspiring in beauty and variety, and with which it is easy to establish a quick rapport. This adds lustre to the procedure of designing, so that far from being dull and dreary and mechanical, the task becomes a pleasant challenge and an absorbing activity.

9

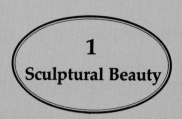

1
Sculptural Beauty

Strips of eucalyptus and other bark, grouped together with a compatible container and base create a satisfying sculptural setting for a few choice flowers. With such a long-lasting framework, the effects can be varied with other attractive additions, because the earthy mellow colours, and the nature of the sculpture will adapt to many other combinations of colour, shape and texture.

The vibrant red of amaryllis is a stunning colour contrast, and the sculptural beauty of the flowers adds design distinction. An orange clivia, or a green, white or yellow lily would look equally dramatic and suit the setting, but a cluster of smaller blooms such as carnations, chrysanthemums or roses would also be quite effective. Sculptural dried seedheads or cones, or dried flowers would complement the bark in colour and texture for a monochromatic scheme when flowers are scarce. Interesting foliage, like a head of croton, or other colourful leaves or succulents could be substituted, and even with nothing added, combined with a vase that has affinity, the effect is pleasing and decorative enough.

I am fortunate in having such a spectacular and ready-made piece of sculpture, and not every sample is perhaps so accommodating in use, but bark is plentiful, and often found around fallen or older trees in fields and woods and road-side or country lanes. Even if there are no eucalyptus trees near you, there are many other sources, even in towns.

Keep your eyes on the pavement, the plane trees in London and elsewhere often shed their bark, and this is very beautiful. The smaller pieces used here to complement the major line of the structure, were in fact picked up in a busy London square. Most city folk are in too great a hurry to pay attention to dedicated collectors like flower arrangers searching for potential props for flower arranging.

Design Analysis

Design impact is established by the strong line and form of the major piece of bark, supported by that of the base and vase.

Since there is an economy of plant material contrasts are definite, with little or no transition of each element to diminish its effectiveness. For instance leaves and additional decoration would have reduced the force of the shape and colour contrast, and beauty of the enclosed space.

There is a pleasing repetition of shape in the pattern of solid and space of the design and that of the vase, and in the outline of the flowers and pointed portions of the bark.

Textures are predominantly smooth and matt, with evident harmony between bark, container and surface of the base. A hint of a glossy surface in the rim of the wooden base reflects the sparkling quality of the flowers. The matt, felt background harmonises with the dominant range of textures. Colour contrasts are pleasingly dramatic, the surface highlights in the bark echo those of the flowers.

Spaces in container, base and structure of the plant material give a rhythmical sequence to the design and add interest to its balance.

The spaces also add a sense of depth, and the flowers are greatly enhanced when framed by the attractive area of enclosed space.

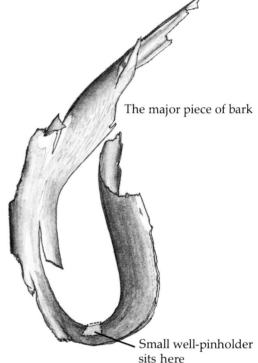

The major piece of bark

Small well-pinholder sits here

Earthy coloured pottery vase with a jagged rim

A polished wooden base turned upside down for a matt surface

The smaller sections of the bark

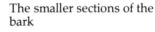

The stability of the base aids balance, but its rhythmic line improves rather than detracts from the movement of design.

The well-pinholder used to anchor and hold water for the flowers serves as an unobtrusive holding device. It is a small sturdy holder in which the pins are permanently fixed as an integral part.

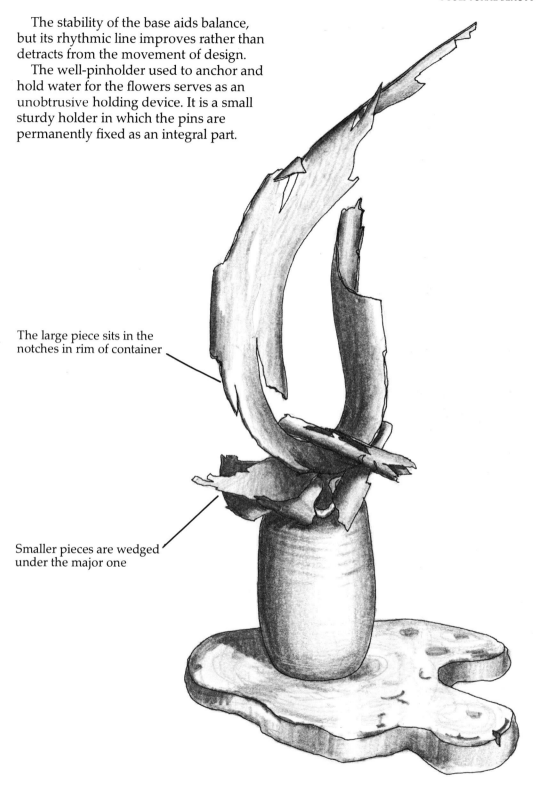

The large piece sits in the notches in rim of container

Smaller pieces are wedged under the major one

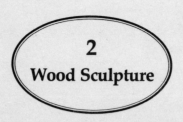

2
Wood Sculpture

A composition based on a similar idea to the preceding arrangement but this is a little more complicated to put together, as it is separate sections of driftwood assembled to look as one. This creates another satisfactory framework of a more permanent nature for presenting ephemeral plants.

You may also have smaller or less spectacular pieces of wood, that can combine together for a more impressive structure. When this more difficult part is mastered, you will have a delicious feeling of achievement with an individual piece of natural sculpture needing just the final artistic touch.

A container or some kind of holding device that adds to the decorative value is recommended, preferably one that helps to stabilise the arrangement. The vase used here is highly satisfactory both from the practical and aesthetic aspect. It has two openings wide enough to give firm anchorage to the slimmer section of the heavier piece of wood which can be wedged safely into these and further stabilised by the solid lower portion of the vase. It is attractively designed with a shape that blends with the line of the wood, and a slight lustre to give a change of texture. The grey-blue colour harmonises with the weathered wood.

The final highlights can be adapted to the seasonal availability of plants or the colours of the setting. The bright pink roses look nice against a pale blue-grey background, and (on the back cover photograph) the gold roses are well contrasted by brown. A black background would dramatise vivid scarlet roses.

Other types of plant material such as fruit and leaves and seedheads could look effective, and each version would create a different composition.

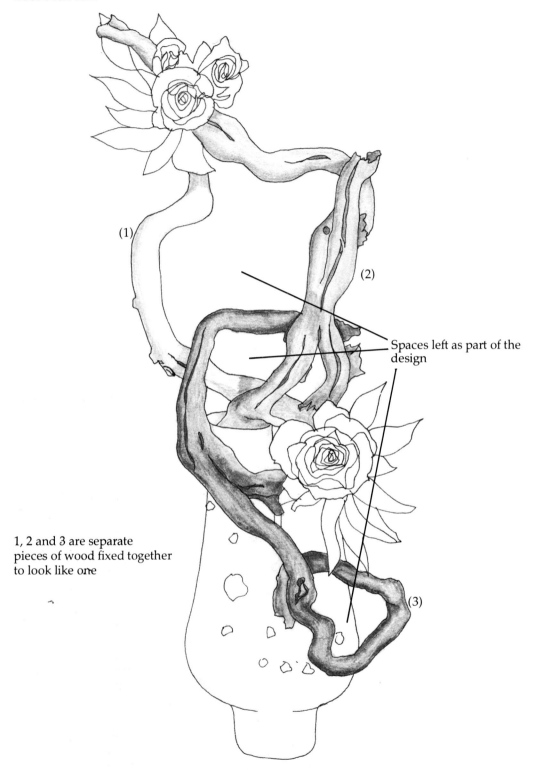

(1)

(2)

Spaces left as part of the design

1, 2 and 3 are separate pieces of wood fixed together to look like one

(3)

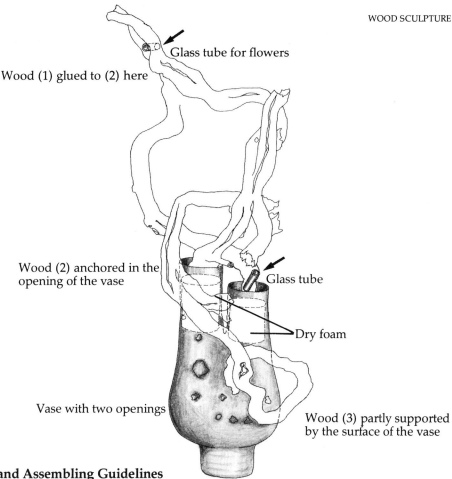

Glass tube for flowers

Wood (1) glued to (2) here

Wood (2) anchored in the
opening of the vase

Glass tube

Dry foam

Vase with two openings

Wood (3) partly supported
by the surface of the vase

Designing and Assembling Guidelines

Clearly assembling the pieces of wood is
the biggest hurdle, which, once mastered
allows ideas to reach fruition. Safe anchorage of all sections to each other and the
complete unit in the container is the
prime consideration. Dry floral foam
packed tightly into the hollowed portions
of the vase gives sufficient stability here.
Heavier subjects might need clay or a
driftwood holder for extra holding power.

The smaller pieces are anchored by the
larger piece and surface of the vase and
tied with fine wire at one or two points of
contact as an extra safety precaution.

The flower stems and leaves are in
small glass tubes of water tied to the
wood or could be in floral foam wrapped
in thin polythene. The tubes must
naturally be topped up when necessary.

It would be interesting to experiment
with different design concepts in
compositions of a similar nature. One
could try a single placement instead of
two or the units could be placed in other
areas of the design to see how this would
affect the rhythm, balance and the space
interest.

Varying the pattern like this would
show the artistic possibilities with one
basic foundation. Whatever presentation
is adopted, clarity of structure should be
preserved and the beauty of wood and
space remain as prominent features.

Experiments with backgrounds of
different colour and texture would also
illustrate the influence of these on the
space element of the design.

3
Modern Decor

This design would suit a modern home or the foyer of a modern hotel or office. It is bold, and clean in line and form, and uses a minimum of plant material in a most dramatic way. Since the material is also very long-lasting, the design is both practical and economical.

The container is a handsome decoration in itself, and being sturdy and substantial, will not topple easily – a great advantage in an area where activity is anticipated. It is very striking in shape, like a piece of modern sculpture, and has an interesting surface featuring both rough and smooth textures. It is made of metal and meant as a lamp base, but with the fittings left out, it functions as a container.

The plant is a bromeliad called Guzmania minor available as house-plants in garden centres, florists and department stores, and their long lasting qualities recommend their use both as growing plants and decorative accent in design.

They can tolerate dry conditions and should not be over-watered, so placing it aloft as I have done here would seem in keeping with requirements. It still has the roots left on – wrapped up in polythene covered with a small cylinder of bark. The plant has panache, and a rather jaunty air, with a hint of the jungle and tropical warmth in its vivid scarlet bracts – guzmanias come from the tropical rain forests, and many are epiphytes which grow on trees. It flowers once only, but after its burst of glory is dimmed, new growths appear at the side, and these can be potted up to make flowers for the following year – all in all, a plant that is a good investment.

Design Analysis

Units are bold and eyecatching through-out, and there is nothing that is super-fluous.

Line is clearly defined with the varied movements of the design combining to create definite rhythm.

The loop of Honeysuckle vine creates a strong diagonal direction, and the piece of driftwood lifts the main placement up into space to give a more dynamic move-ment and added space interest.

There is repetition of form between the pattern of the container and the shape of the enclosed space made by the vine. The round shapes in the vase are similarly defined in the centre of the Guzmania.

The textures of the vase are harmonised or contrasted with the polished driftwood, the vine lightly sprayed with bronze metallic paint and with the semi-glossy leaves of the plant.

The visual weight of the container is offset by the space enclosed by the loop of vine, the space above the rim of the vase, and by the colourful rosette.

Whilst there is not a lot of colour, this is sharply contrasted, and is affected by the colour of the setting. Here, against a brown background, the bromeliad is thrown into strong relief.

Technique

This is not an easy 'container' to fix the components in, as the opening is rather small and there is no flat surface to work on inside. I found a piece of driftwood that exactly fitted into the hole and was held there firmly. The bottom of the vine loop is wedged into the container for safety, and the top rests on the wood.

The plant material rests on the wood, stabilised by the grip of the vine.

The polythene prevents the roots from being dried out and these should be inspected now and then and moistened if necessary. Most plants (and flowers) will tolerate a dry atmopshere but situations where there is a howling draught or very strong sunlight should be avoided.

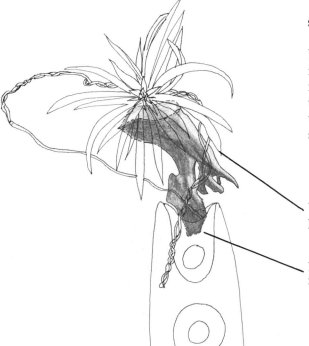

Wood supports twig and plant here

Driftwood and twig wedged into opening of vase

Drawing illustrates the distinctive features of each item

Twig with an attractive
silhouette

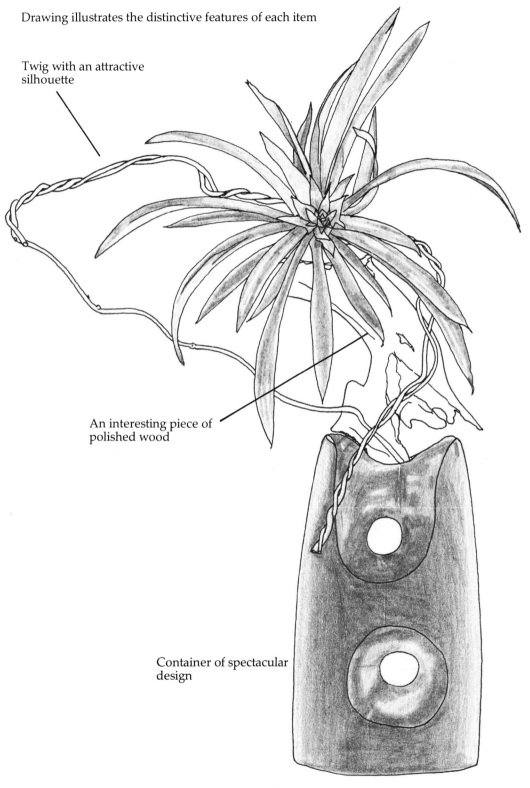

An interesting piece of
polished wood

Container of spectacular
design

4
Creative Design

The flower arranger works within a wide spectrum of rich visual forms from the extravagant palette of Nature. Yet comparatively little is needed to create or interpret these images in a flower arrangement. A few crisp lines, a texture sufficiently assertive, or the merest touch of a luscious colour can in miniature represent the splendour of nature's wider canvas.

The modern designer learns to be selective and discriminating, on the principle that a frugal design needs some distinctive touch, either in the material used, or its presentation.

Happily success does not always depend on finding something rare and exotic or using what is very costly. It is governed more by observation, and developing the ability to spot the unusual or of seeing the commonplace in relation to its design possibilities.

It is then the skill of the designer in combining shape with line and space, harmonising colours and displaying strange and beautiful textures that gives design distinction.

When not working to a preconceived formula or a set plan, it is easier to be guided by the nature of the material, and to let the design evolve its own pattern. The shape of a branch or a striking texture or colour can often influence the design approach, and a subtle combination of these elements might be the means of design distinction. Modern containers also encourage originality, as they can often be used in novel ways to enhance the special qualities of the plant material or to present this in new and imaginative ways.

It is the freedom of outlook and procedure that makes creative designing so stimulating, and gives constant opportunity to make fresh discoveries and to develop new ideas.

Drawing to illustrate the major lines
which create the rhythm of the arrangement

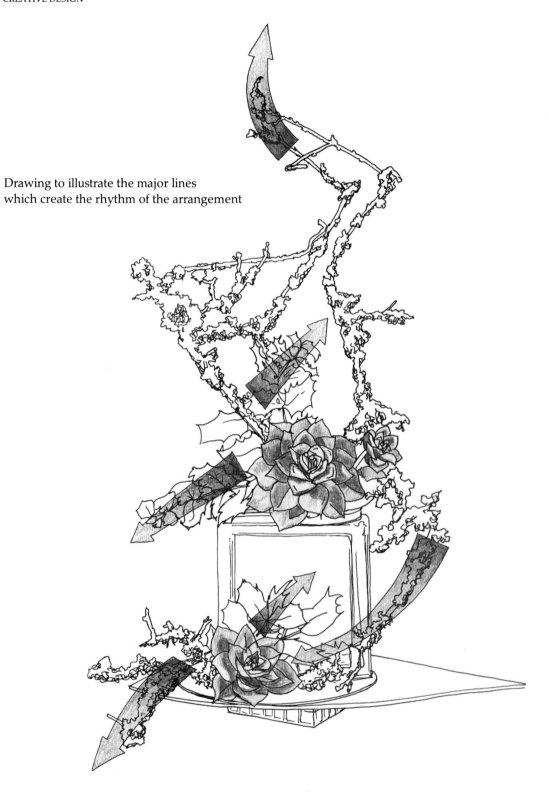

Design Comments

There are just three types of plant material used here, but each has a distinctive shape, colour or texture to make an interesting design.

Textural contrast is a strong feature, with the hoary roughness of the lichen emphasised by the smooth, matt succulents and shiny berberis leaves. The glass brick and acrylic base provide another distinct contrast.

There is an attractive colour contrast also, with soft blue-grey hues highlighted by the russet tints and tones.

The lichened branches inspired the format of the design, with their line and space elements suggesting the pattern of the arrangement. There are several lines of movement, the topmost twig takes the eye in a vertical path, the lowest placement moves forward. The two separate groups of plant material activate the rhythm also, and help to diminish the dominance of the container and base. The leaves and succulents with their own line of movement also aid the overall rhythm of the design.

There are distinct contrasts of form in the pronounced roundness of the succulents, serrated surfaces of the leaves, irregular form of the branches, and in the pattern of the container and base.

Further Details

Assembling the design is straightforward. Two small glass dishes holding pinholders are placed at the two levels to anchor the material.

Diagram shows the contrast of form

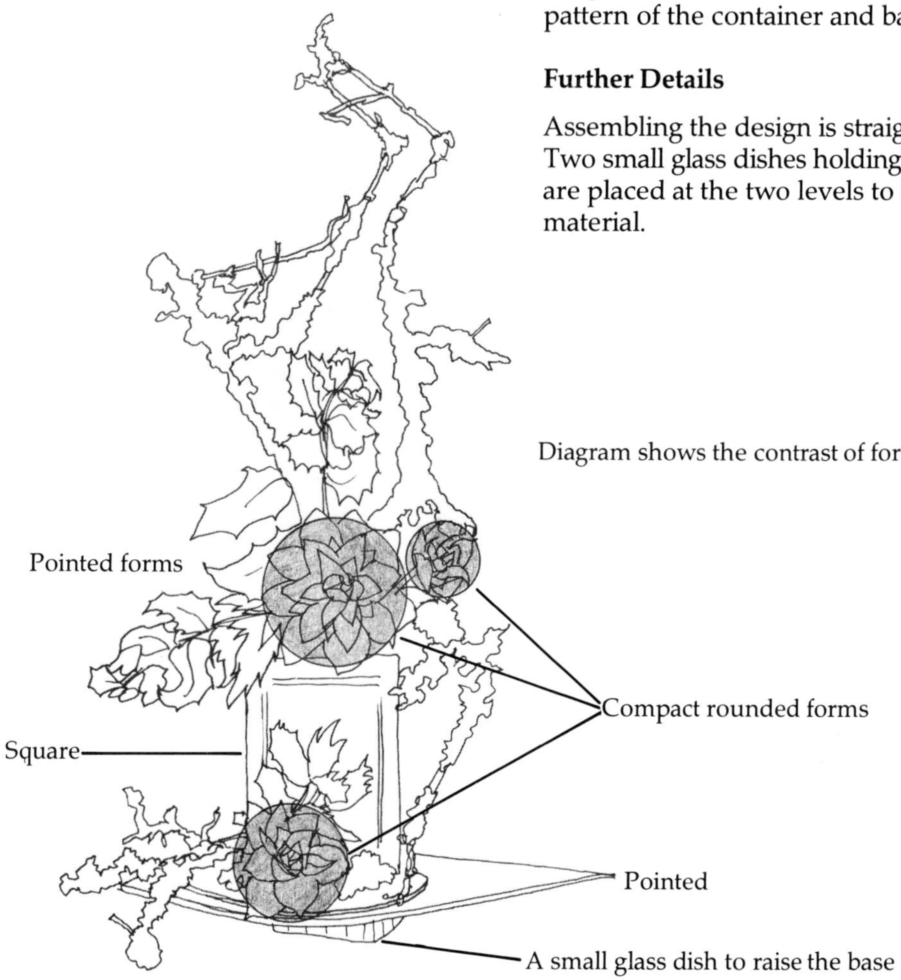

Pointed forms

Compact rounded forms

Square

Pointed

A small glass dish to raise the base

5
A Long-lasting Arrangement

This type of arrangement has both modern and traditional design characteristics. It could be called a line-mass, as there is more plant material used than in the very streamlined, sparse design, but line is still a feature and a positive element.

It would be a refreshing decoration for the home, as it is not over-dramatic and displays crisp, trim plant material that is long-lasting. The belladonna lily (*Amaryllis belladona*) is an enchanting flower with its pink trumpets borne in clusters at the head of an attractive, purplish-brown stem. It is an easy flower to arrange, for the stem is sturdy and solid to insert on a pinholder – an endearing attribute as so many flower stems split or splay on the pins.

Flowers are individual like people, some are bold and showy and extroverted and these act best as solo performers. Others are more retiring and less spectacular. Many can be called beautiful, or lovely, charming, elegant or glorious. Some we tend to regard as practical, useful or accommodating, but very few as nasty, really ugly or disgusting; though some are awkward, wilful, and unpredictable. The designer considers these special attributes in relation to the aims of the design.

The lilies here are combined with *Phormium tenax* – New Zealand flax, in both the variegated and the purple variety. This is a most useful foliage, which can be used in so many different ways. It is excellent for giving height and an architectural quality to an arrangement, and it is easy to alter its natural form into new shapes and line. The other leaves are borrowed from a house-plant – *Rhoeo discolor*, better known as the boat lily on account of its small boat-shaped flowers. These, however are rather insignificant and of little use in flower arranging, but the fleshy strap-shaped leaves are very handsome. They are green and cream above and a rich purple underneath to match the flax and flowers.

Detail of technique

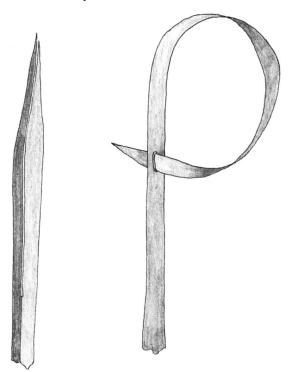
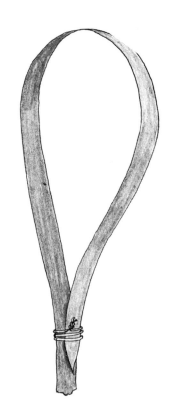

Design Analysis

The straight spears of the *phormium* create a strong vertical line for the centre of the design. The circular loops define the dimensions of the arrangement on the right, and the other leaves perform a similar function on the left.

The flowers are spaced to give clarity to their line and form with some of the *phormium* loops used to modify the regularity of the placements. The circular shapes also improve the rhythm and depth of the design generally, and break up the solidity with space areas.

Balance is asymmetrical and conventionally organised, though there is no heavy or static focal area. The accessories which balance the height proportions are visually light and rhythmical.

Textures are predominantly smooth with matt, semi-glossy, and shiny surfaces. The background of felt is a duller matt texture. There is sufficient colour contrast to be interesting, with tints, shades and tones harmonising pleasantly rather than contrasting dramatically.

The dark blue-grey of the background accentuates the pink of the flowers, and the colours of the arrangement are echoed in the glass accessories.

Technical Details

Stems were stabilised by a pinholder in a small bowl on the two glass bases.

Phormium loops are made by splitting the spear down the centre, the tip is then pushed through a small slit lower in the stem.

Alternatively ends can be tied together with thread or thin wire.

28

In the black and white version, form and line and the organisation of the units are clearly defined

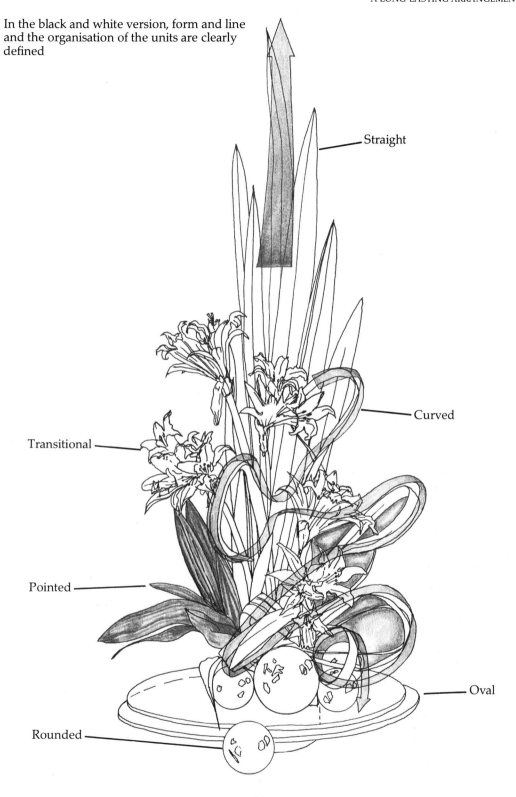

Straight

Curved

Transitional

Pointed

Oval

Rounded

6
Flamingo Flower

A variation on the previous design, following a very similar pattern, using different flowers.

The anthurium, or flamingo flower, makes an alluring contribution to a sparse arrangement, with its intriguing shape, bright colour, and sophisticated texture. It is an eye-catching flower that compels many an onlooker at a flower show to touch the shiny, plastic-like surface to see whether this is real – a practice guaranteed to annoy the exhibitor who has probably paid a lot for each bloom, for alas, in a temperate climate, they need a hot-house and so are expensive to buy.

Their cost however, is offset by excellent lasting qualities, and like other, showy, exotic flowers, such as strelitzia (Bird of Paradise flower) or heliconia (Lobster Claw), a couple, or one even makes quite an impression.

The supporting material here is also very durable, to make a long-lasting framework for whatever flowers are available. The arrangement based on a straightforward pattern of a vertical and horizontal line, is easily put together, using a few basic shapes in plant material. These can be varied with different selections that suit and harmonise with each other or provide contrast. The height of the arrangement for example, could be established with other tall, pointed subjects like yucca, sansevieria, or iris leaves. Reedmace, teasle, verbascum or onopordum spikes, kniphofia, eremurus, molucella, acanthus, would also create a strong, vertical line. The broader leaves could be substituted by bergenea, hosta, arum leaves, or those of verbascum, onopordum, and cardoon. Any flower of good form, and harmonising colour would link together these, and other combinations.

Fruit could replace the glass accessories, or the flowers. There are infinite groupings of form, texture and colour possible from the wide range of plants, that would be pleasant to plan and put together.

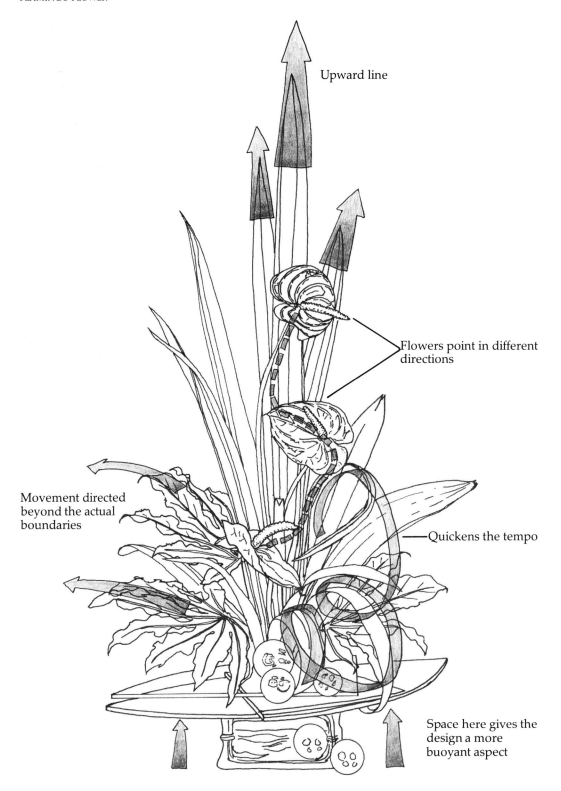

Upward line

Flowers point in different directions

Movement directed beyond the actual boundaries

Quickens the tempo

Space here gives the design a more buoyant aspect

32

Design Comments

The units are conventionally put together to radiate from a central area in a traditional manner. Transitional material is however kept to a minimum so that the elements remain sharply contrasted, and the units well defined.

The use of a pinholder, as opposed to the more bulky floral foam, helps to keep the central area uncluttered.

The silhouette is also crisp and clear, with no superfluous outline material.

The bold, spear-like phormium leaves are well contrasted by the form of the broader fatsia.

The spadix of the anthurium repeats the pointed shapes, whilst the softer accessories provide contrast.

The glass ornaments, container and base also harmonise in texture with the shiny spathes. The roughness of the spadix contrasts with the smooth, matt, and semi-glossy foliage.

Red and green make a complementary colour harmony, but the differing values of the green hue, and touches of cream and yellow modify the harsh contrast.

The vertical line of the phorium creates an ascending rhythm whilst the contours of the broad leaves and those of the transitional clivia foliage direct movement into wider dimensions.

The circular line of the phormium loops enlivens the tempo, and improves the space interest in the structures of the design. The tips of the anthurium centres 'moving' in definable directions, and the placement of each bloom creates a sequence of movement also.

Space organised around each item again aids design depth and rhythm, and prevents too solid an effect.

Balance is organised along conventional lines, though the central focus of the design is not over-emphasised, and the units though visually balanced are assembled for a dynamic effect.

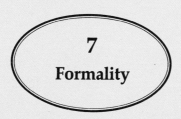

7
Formality

Having discussed a few modern ideas, and looked at some modern arrangements, examples of the more traditional style are included next for the interest of comparison and consideration of the principles of design applicable to these examples.

The arrangements are based on traditional patterns, but they embrace some of the modern concepts also, with old and new principles intermingling.

The first example is a familiar triangular arrangement of soft, flowing line, but streamlined to a more modern version.

This is a flower lover's design, the gardener's delight, as it is a splendid way of displaying plant material in as naturalistic a way as possible.

Without the softening influence of a few treasures from the garden, this type of arrangement can look a little stiff and very formal as it is the curve of stem or tendril and slight horticultural imperfections that add the touch of informality and charm.

In large displays, the arranger can really let go, and select a rich variety of colour, form and texture for a lavish mass. This is a smaller version using a modest amount of material in a controlled design, but it still displays a fair variety of plant shapes and colour and the items are all from the garden.

The outline is made of ballota, atriplex, ivy, and sprays of hops which are good for trailing over the edge of the vase for a softer line. Central interest is provided by pale mauve roses, and cream yucca flowers. The leaves used as transition are those of green and white hosta and Helleborus foetidus. The container is of pewter which harmonises with the soft hues of the arrangement.

Design Observation

The arrangement follows the conventional pattern, with the material radiating from one central area.

Rhythm is formal, with the fine material drawing the eye outward from the centre to the outer dimensions.

Light and dark values of colour also help the rhythm.

Balance is conventional with equal visual weight either side of the central axis, but this is achieved with different material.

An over-weighted focal area however is avoided to keep the design rhythmical. The proportions of the arrangement are conventional. Textures are varied, ballota, atriplex and hops are rough, roses are silky, yucca blooms smooth and matt, hosta is ribbed, ivy leaves have a slight sheen which reflect light. The pewter container has a dull metallic surface.

Colours advance and recede, but blend and harmonise rather than perform strong contrasts.

Space – though not a pronounced feature, is organised to give clarity to the plant material throughout the arrangement. Mechanics are conventional, with a round of water-retaining foam in a candle cup secured to the top of the stand.

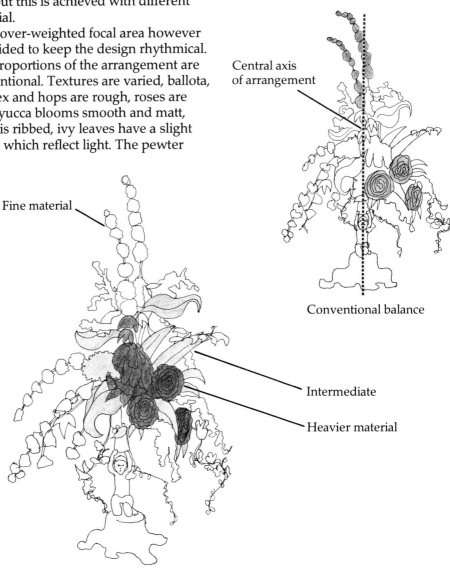

Central axis of arrangement

Conventional balance

Fine material

Intermediate

Heavier material

A traditional way of
assembling

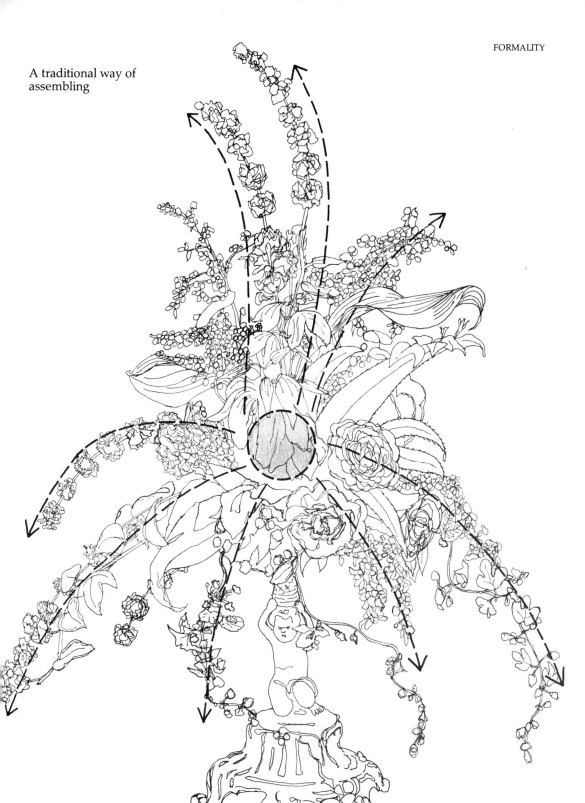

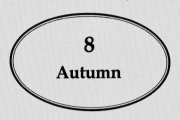

8
Autumn

A larger fuller mass arrangement with autumn or late summer gleanings from hedgerow and garden.

Colours are brighter, textures richer and shapes more varied than in the previous arrangement as autumn is a time of fruitful plenty and galaxy of colour. But here also, there is a controlled line in the design, and careful placing to display each item.

There are only a few flowers used, with interest extended to other forms of plant life at varying stages of development. Seedheads of reedmace and their attractive strap leaves and velvety texture, large *Arum italicum pictum* seedheads, some green, others bright orange-red. What a fantastic tactile quality they have, echoed in the sprays of wild berries from the hedgerow, (or was it garden, for mine, adjoining farmland and fields, is I regret to say rather full of weeds). My gardening help calls this particular one the sweetheart plant because of its compulsive habit of embracing every tree and shrub it encounters. It is a nuisance weed, that seems to grow a mile a minute, but an attractive one, though one would hesitate to use the berries with young children around.

The green and gold variegated dogwood (*Cornus spaethii*) is a refreshing colour contrast to the darker *Berberis acquifolium* leaves, two of which have been preserved – the other matches the bright red of the pepper.

The pretty leaf in front of the largest rudbeckia is that of clematis, while strips of plane tree bark complete the structure of the design and carry through the colour repetition of the reedmace in their tints and shades of brown.

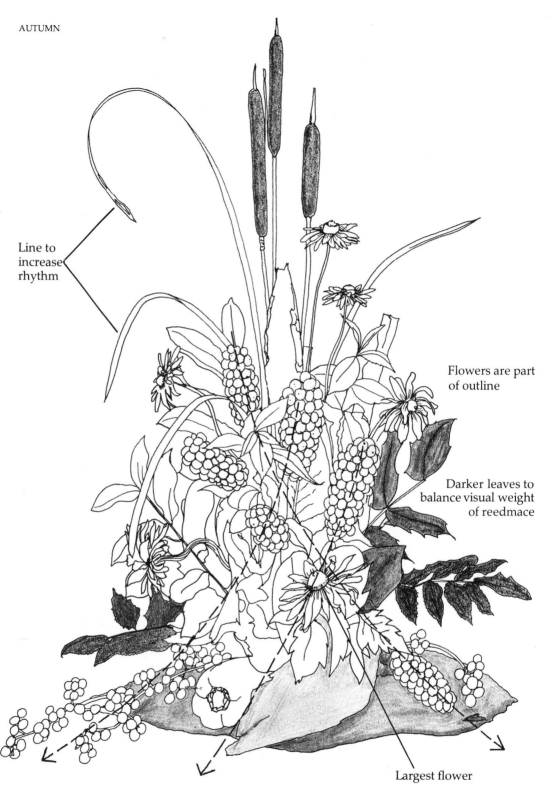

Line to
increase
rhythm

Flowers are part
of outline

Darker leaves to
balance visual weight
of reedmace

Largest flower

Material placed to take the eye smoothly through the design structure

Design Comments

Though there is a fairly varied selection of material used, items are grouped and rhythmically placed for a harmonious presentation. The seedheads, for instance have a definite line of movement that takes the eye through the body of the design and its dimensions.

The line of the flowers define these boundaries too, and the largest brings the eye into the centre. None of the blooms are presented entirely full face as they are rather a dominant shape.

The reedmace at the top might have made the design top-heavy, but the brown leaves, bark, and base counter this through colour repetition, and so help the balance of the arrangement. (See diagram).

The foliage of the reedmace improves the rhythm and creates more design space. The topmost one defines an attractive and eyecatching area which animates the design considerably. The larger flower and darker leaves balance this on the opposite side.

Textures are rich and varied, bullrushes are velvety, with repetition of this texture in the centre of the flowers. Bark is smooth and matt, the base rough and matt. Contrast lies in the shiny red pepper and the berries.

Colours are predominantly warm, with the greenery for contrast. Shapes are the traditional selection of round, pointed, and intermediate forms.

Eye-catching line and area of space

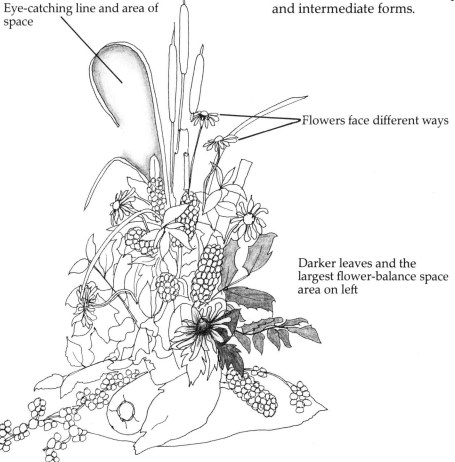

Flowers face different ways

Darker leaves and the largest flower-balance space area on left

41

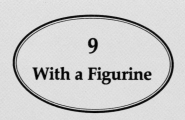

9
With a Figurine

A composition built around a bronze figure which has an attractive
shape and very rhythmical line.
As the various features are so distinctive, they guided the choice of
plant material and type of arrangement that would suit and enhance
its characteristics.
It is a traditional type ornament that I acquired in my early days of
flower arranging when it was still possible to find such objects. They
were very popular then used as accessories or made into a container,
and most arrangers of that era tried to own one. Today, when
interpretations tend not to be so literal the modern designer, myself
included, tends to ignore these realistic females. Once in a while
however, they can again participate in a semi-naturalistic setting, in
designs that basically are traditional, but have a stronger accent on line.
My lady is in a formal setting of a traditional type picture frame, and the
arrangement follows the conventional shape and concept. The design
however, is controlled to give a more strongly defined outline and
lighter rhythm than a full-bodied mass. It demonstrates again, how
space can replace large quantities of plant material. By incorporating
voids that have beauty and interest, the number of solid items needed
are reduced, for space performs the same positive role. When selecting
the units to be used, think of space as something actual, and not
a negative item. Say to yourself, here are my leaves, flowers, fruits or
whatever, and I must also have a small/large, round/oval or free-form
area of space as certain points of interest. Apart from modifying the
massed effect, space will improve the rhythm of the arrangement, and
make its balance far more interesting. Alternatively assemble the plant
material, then stand some distance away, and study the pattern made.
Assess the ratio of solid to space, often removing one flower or leaf,
and leaving a void can transform the design quality and character
of the composition.
Working within positively defined dimensions, like a picture frame,
surrounding space greatly enhances the picture.

Design Assessment

Proportioning the composition to its setting is obviously a major consideration. Notice the space left above the top line of the arrangement and at each side.

The scale of an accessory to the arrangement is an important factor also, to the overall dimensions and separate items used. Placements must be planned so the figurine does not dominate, and its line falls into the dominant rhythm and pattern of the design for a unified effect.

The figurine here is placed to the side and rear of the arrangement, but is united with it through the line and pattern of the twigs and general direction of the plant material. (See diagram.)

The visual weight of the figure to the left is balanced by the dominant colour and shape of the hemerocallis (Day lily) to the right and the important space areas created by the twigs.

Depth and rhythm is also aided by the rhythmic line and enclosed voids.

There is textural and colour harmony between the branches and the figure, with the smooth, satiny day lily giving the major contrast.

Colours are complementary, but as these are tints, shades, and tones of yellow and purple, the contrast is modified, and softened with the grey-green foliage.

Technical Details and Illustrations

Frame is free-standing, with metal brackets fixed to each side. A rectangle of wood rests on this for added stability.

As it is not 'boxed' in it needs to stand against a clear background.

The figure is on its own stand – hidden by the plant material.

An extra base lifts the arrangement above the edge of the frame.

Plant material is in plastic foam in a small dish.

Space left between top of arrangement and frame

Wooden base

Metal brackets

Showing the proportions of figure to arrangement and arrangement to the dimensions of the frame

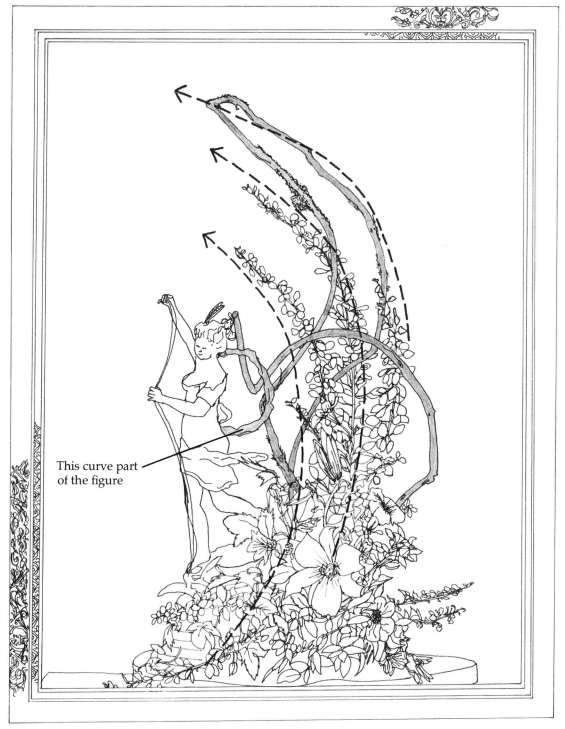

This curve part of the figure

Drawing to show how the line of the plant material follows that of the figurine and how the curving twigs repeat the figurine's decorative aspects

45

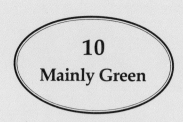

10
Mainly Green

There are many different greens in nature and it is such a refreshing colour, that all-green, or mainly green arrangements are tremendously popular. With the numerous range of green foliage, fruits and even flowers, the arranger can create attractive compositions with sufficient variation of hue as well as of texture and shape.

Green flowers have the appeal of something unusual. Green zinnia for instance, or gladiolus, the green arum lily, seem more special than the commonly coloured versions. Viridiflora tulips and roses, hydrangea, euphorbia, some of the hellebores, are other green, or mainly green flowers or bracts. *Viburnum opulus* 'Sterile' is a delightful pale green when the rounded ball like flowers first appear and molucella (Bells of Ireland), or the enchanting green *Cobaea scandens,* must be among the top favourites. The green kniphofia used here is also very attractive in colour and texture and makes a slim graceful line.

Sprays of winter jasmine foliage provide a dainty outline material, contrasted by strap-like *Iris foetidissima,* and tapered oval of aspidistra leaves, with *Fatsia japonica* adding another distinctive shape.

Fruit and vegetables, of edible and non-edible varieties can also contribute shape and texture, and there are many green varieties depending on the stage of plant development. The lush green berries of *Arum italicum pictum* are very decorative. My plants are so prolific, they have virtually taken over part of the garden, and the pretty marbled leaves are king-sized too. The pale green sheaths that appear before the berries are another bonus, so one could not possibly begrudge it house room.

The final highlight is from the two beautiful rosettes of a choice rhododendron foliage, which are as decorative as any flowers, and last much longer.

In fact, the whole arrangement lasted ages, and the berries turned from green to red before the leaves showed any signs of wilting. The kniphofia was still quite decorative, even when the florets faded.

Design Analysis

This is a fairly traditional type of design with the units organised to radiate from a conventional centre. Three types of plants were used, visually heavier in the middle, with the lighter material drawing the eye outwards to the edge of the arrangement, and transitional material for a controlled and gentle rhythm from shape to shape, size to size.

These pointed, round and oval forms give the necessary contrast and variety for design appeal and interest.

Textures range from the roughly formed flowers to the smooth, shiny surfaces of the berries and pepper, with those of the leaves offered as transition. The clear acrylic bases harmonise with the light reflecting textures, the matt background with the duller elements. Colours are mainly monochromatic, with tints of analogous hues. Background adds emphasis through repetition.

The line of the design is soft and flowing guided by the nature of the material, and its most prominent movement. The broader leaves of fatsia and aspidistra add to the depth illusion, and pointed material promotes the rhythm.

The balance is asymmetrical, with the longer line of the jasmine and forward movement of the kniphofia stem on the left, balanced by the pull of the shorter, broader fatsia leaf and greater distribution of flowers on the right.

Again, the visual weight of the rhododendron, greater on the left, is balanced by more berries on the right side of the central axis.

A large pinholder placed in a glass dish anchors the stems.

Diagram to show the contrasting forms used

Longer line of design

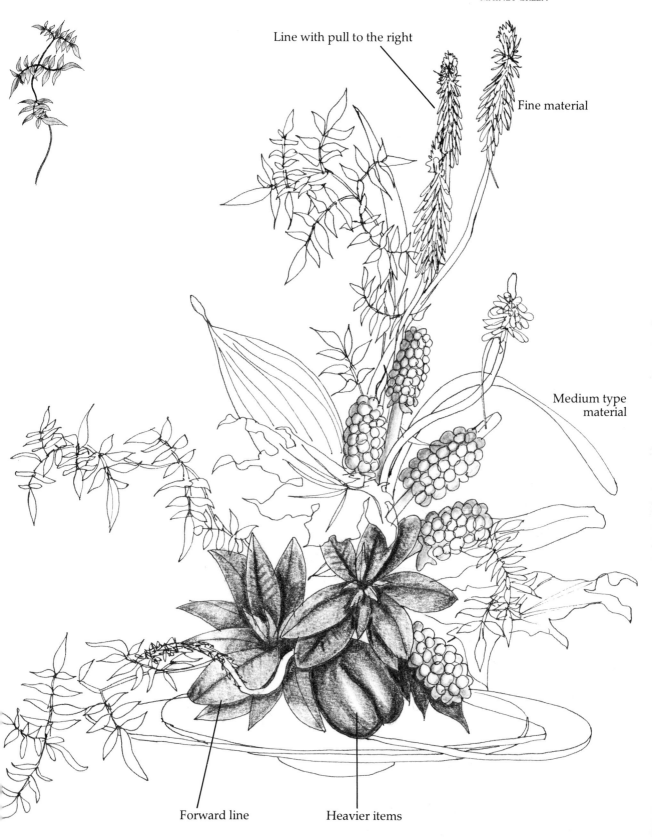

Line with pull to the right

Fine material

Medium type material

Forward line

Heavier items

11
Inspired by 'Still-Life'

The term 'still-life' brings to mind the Dutch and Flemish paintings of the seventeenth century. These are superb compositions of visual richness, that are a delight to look at and to study. They illustrate how the shape of different objects, their surface quality and colour, can be combined in total harmony. The skill of these masters has captured on canvas the beauty of flowers seen in profile, with stem and structure clearly emphasised. It is interesting also to see how the solidity of form of certain objects is contrasted with graceful, trailing plants or tendrils.

Flower arrangers today can draw on inspiration from the past, and adapt the concepts and principles to designs using plant material with allied objects. This extends the opportunity of displaying shape, form, colour and texture of flowers, fruits and leaves in new relationships for rich and interesting compositions.

Like the painter, the flower arranger can combine the natural with attractive ornaments, whether a precious heirloom or just a pretty trinket. Kitchenware can be most attractive, and has a natural affinity with fruits and herbs and vegetables. Trugs and baskets, and small garden ornaments are also very suitable with garden plants and produce. Shells and fossils, lobster pots and fishing nets combined with plants around the sea shore and driftwood could portray a marine theme. Sophisticated objects would need more elegant flowers and leaves of harmonising textures, a Dresden figurine and fine china, the complement of choice or delicate flowers.

The main essential is to achieve harmony in the finished composition. This is not based on a typical arrangement of flowers in the conventional sense, but just a positioning of different objects combined to give visual pleasure and an interesting study. It is a stimulating field of research, and it can foster greater awareness of the make-up of flower, fruit, and leaf seen in new associations.

Design Observation

As explained, this style is not just a *flower* arrangement, but associated groupings of plants with other objects, arranged to enhance each other. The composition here is built around the two Victorian pewter urns, one standing upright, the other turned on its side, to form the major line of the design. This is accentuated by the two placements of fruit to define a pleasing curve. Trailing stems of clematis and hop unite the objects and draw the eye through the design and give the contrast of lighter material. The flowers, colourful berries and textured cloth placed left of the central line of the design balance the visual weight of the larger quantity of fruit and second accessory on the right. Texture is a strong feature, and there is variety in flowers, leaves, fruits and accessories, where smooth, matt, rough and shiny surfaces contrast and blend for a rich visual effect.

Shapes are grouped to give strong emphasis to the distinctive character of each object, and placed where form and other qualities can be most fully appreciated. Each group has individual importance as a focus of interest that is not so markedly merged as in a conventional flower arrangement. The design is based more on the still-life concept where the individual objects, though united, retain their identity.

Illustrations

Top ewer lifted on a box – which also supports the lower one. A small well-pinholder placed at the back of the ewer on the box holds water. The ends of the berried sprays have the ends wrapped in polythene holding a little foam.

Diagram to show how the different groups are organised

52

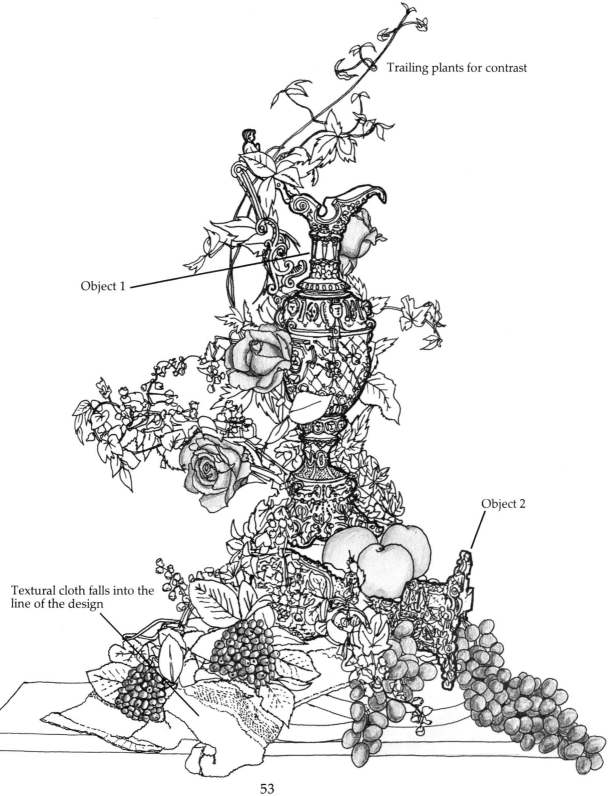

Trailing plants for contrast

Object 1

Object 2

Textural cloth falls into the
line of the design

53

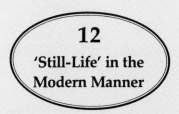

12

'Still-Life' in the Modern Manner

Still-life as applied to flower arranging is not one definite style, as this more modern version demonstrates. Its concept, as in a painting, can take many forms of presentation.

In every period of art, the tendency is to create artistically in relation to the popular objects and trends in style typical of the times. The Dutch and Flemish paintings of the seventeenth and eighteenth centuries display flowers, fruits and vegetables lavishly grouped with stuffed birds and animals or hunting trophies, or items from the dining table. A cubist painter of the twentieth century like Braque, on the other hand, arranges objects of a still life in a more geometric pattern, with fragments or abstractions from the objects to make up the picture. Surrealist painters moving into the subconscious would use objects as they might exist in dreams. Pop artists bring together items of everyday use into assemblages or still-life tableaux that are sometimes humorous or absurd and often controversial.

Whatever form the still-life takes, the objects are seldom merged into a single unit. They are integrated as groups, but retain individuality. Blue-green glassware from Malta inspired the design here staged on glass blocks and a piece of clear acrylic – all modern materials which give a range of sophisticated textures and suave shapes. This composition is in contrast to the previous example in character and content.

Drawing shows how the staging
clearly displays the character
of each object

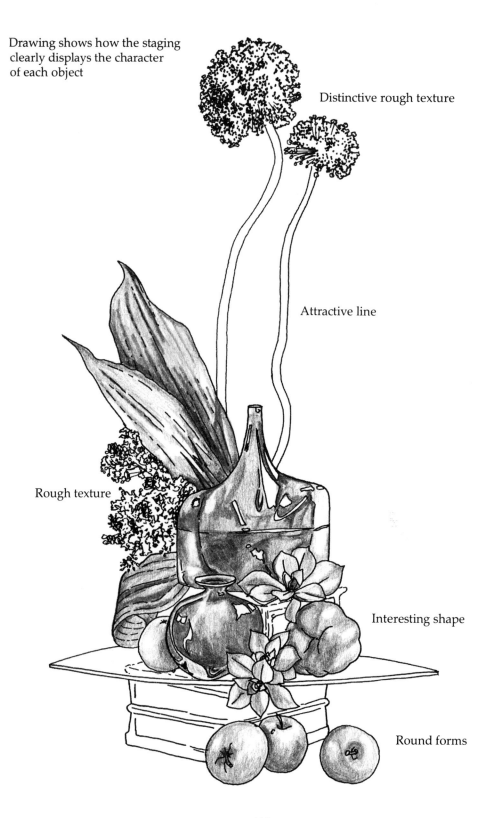

Distinctive rough texture

Attractive line

Rough texture

Interesting shape

Round forms

56

Design Analysis

Plant material and the allied items, though separate entities, are tied together through texture and colour repetition.

The blue-green and yellow-green of the glass-ware is promoted throughout the design, starting from the pale green stems of the leeks, and ending with the yellow-green of the apples.

The rue is blue green like some of the succulents.

Background is a tint of the colour scheme of the arrangement.

There are shiny textures in the aspidistra leaves and fruit, glass and acrylic, with contrast in the rough rue and leeks' seedheads. Succulents are matt and smooth.

The tall line of the leeks and the space area they enclose, balance the weight of the accessories, and emphasise the line of the larger ornament.

The line of the acrylic base gives a contrasting movement and helps to define the lower placement of fruit. The space below

enhances presentation – an important aspect of the composition. By staging objects on different levels, there is a pleasant rhythmic sequence from one to the other. The form of each item is clearly defined – so it is easy to appreciate the individuality of shapes, and to assess the harmony and contrast presented.

Other Details

The units are grouped at different levels on blocks of clear glass, separated by a thin base of acrylic.

A small container hidden behind the ornament holds water for plants needing moisture.

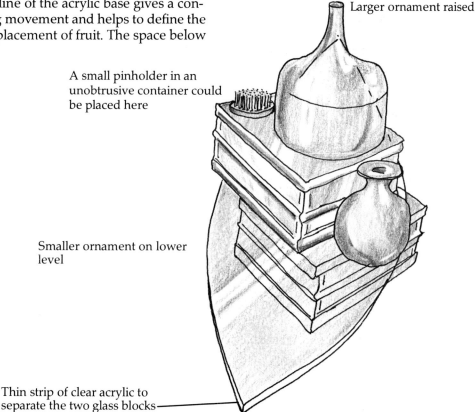

Larger ornament raised

A small pinholder in an unobtrusive container could be placed here

Smaller ornament on lower level

Thin strip of clear acrylic to separate the two glass blocks

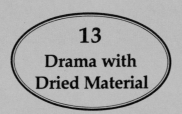

13
Drama with Dried Material

Dried or preserved plant material is of enormous value in modern design. There are none of the limitations set by living plants which need moisture of some kind, so there is greater freedom of presentation. It is also easier to alter the appearance of the material to suit the effect required.

This sculptural composition of dried and preserved palm leaves illustrates the effectiveness of form and texture of the material in this form. Some of the leaves are dried, others preserved in a solution of glycerine and water for a subtle variation of colour.

There is quite a tale to these leaves which might interest you. It all started with an enormous palm tree in the local botanical gardens, that was steadily threatening its way through the roof. It had to be cut down and I was offered some of the leaves, an offer which I accepted without hesitation. I had no idea then though of the dimensions involved, for each one was some four or five feet across and taller than myself. Before even contemplating how to use them, I had to do some very drastic pruning, and split each one down the centre rib. It was like being in a jungle for the number received was more than generous and I was soon knee-deep in verdurous confusion and periodically ravaged by fierce spines that adjoined the woody stems.

It was all worthwhile however for I ended up with a marvellous selection of shapes and varying sizes to design with. A few of the stems were put immediately in the glycerine solution; they take at least three or four weeks to turn brown, but are then preserved for ever.

The palm leaves last for ages in fresh arrangments and later dry naturally to a soft, dull green. These are a year old, and still in fine condition. The wispy hair-like strands are not cobwebs I hasten to add, but thin, hair-like filaments, attached to the leaves, that add further decorative interest.

Design Observation

You may have found from experience, that very often it is difficult to add further interest to a dramatic outline without detracting from its force and impact.

These palm leaves have a very powerful line, which creates the rhythm of the design and makes a very attractive outline yet it was necessary to have something at their point of contact to unify the placements. A strong contrast of colour seemed to hold the eye and interrupt the rhythm. Colour repetition on the other hand blended in and the rounded forms of the seedpods added rather than detracted from the rhythm. These also bring the necessary contrast of form to the design and their darker, hollow, centres make a less solid area of emphasis. Dark and light values of colour throughout the design also help to generate depth and movement. The eye catching line and form of the topmost leaf is balanced by the seed-pods, placed off-centre, and the vigorous line of the palm on the left.

Lack of transitional material in this area also brings the element of space to activate the design and this in turn affects the balance – with spaces on the left countering the more solid aspect on the right. (See diagram.)

The pleated effect of the leaves has a very pronounced textural quality, contrasted by the smoothness of the seedpods and matt finish of the pottery container. This harmonises well with the colour variation in the palm and pods.

Technique

A block of dry plastic foam inside the vase holds the main stems, the lower and side leaves are anchored by openings in the rim of the container – conveniently structured to do just this.

The palm leaf sections were trimmed for a variety of line and pattern.

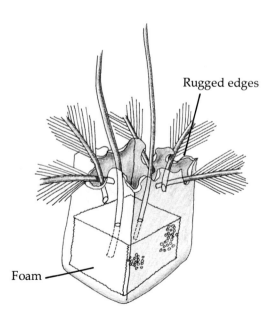

Rugged edges

Foam

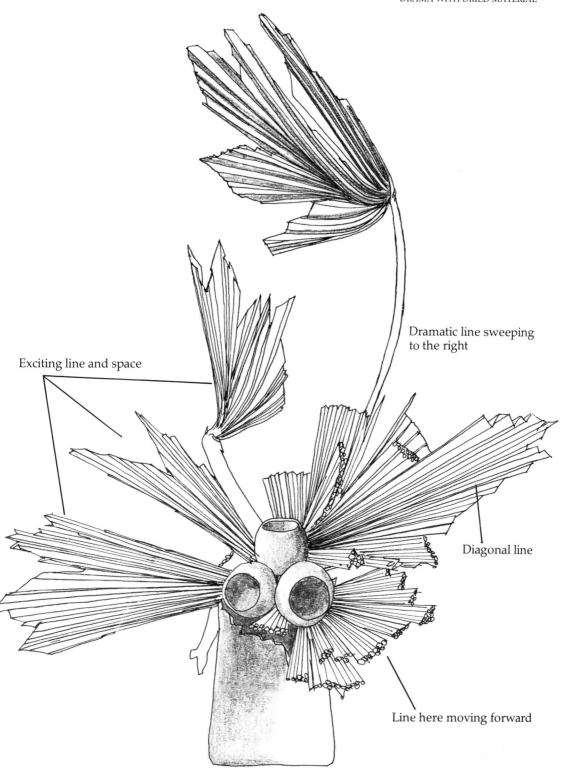

Dramatic line sweeping
to the right

Exciting line and space

Diagonal line

Line here moving forward

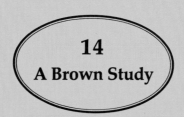

14
A Brown Study

Another arrangement in monochrome which gives full value to the structural beauty of dried or preserved plant material. As in the last arrangement we are made aware of how effective sculptural qualities and textural prominence can be without the support of bright colour. Fresh and dried material do of course combine well together, and one can greatly enhance the other through distinct contrast. The designer is influenced mostly by the effect required and as this is a variable, so are the number of harmonies possible. It would not be wrong to have a strong colour contrast here, it would merely change the accent of the design, which now plays up to line and shape and texture.

Leaves were the inspiration here also, and their special qualities the pivot of the design. This is a tropical foliage plant and the leaves were fresh and green when first acquired. Their very rarity in a temperate climate prompted me to preserve them for future use. There is something very noble and dignified in their line and form, and to give more prominence to texture, I have displayed the back of the leaves where the ribbed surfaces can be more fully appreciated.

Something less solid was needed to complete the outline, and the circles made with strips of wood shavings spark up the tempo without hiding the leaves.

The lotus seedpods repeat the circular forms with another interesting round shape. These are fascinating with their pitted surfaces and the odd seed rattling inside. According to the Oxford English Dictionary, the lotus is represented in ancient Greek legend as 'inducing luxurious dreaminess and distaste for active life'. The Indian water plant with large pink flowers is also of symbolic significance in Hinduism and Buddhism. I think the seedheads are a surprising contrast to the water-lily like flowers.

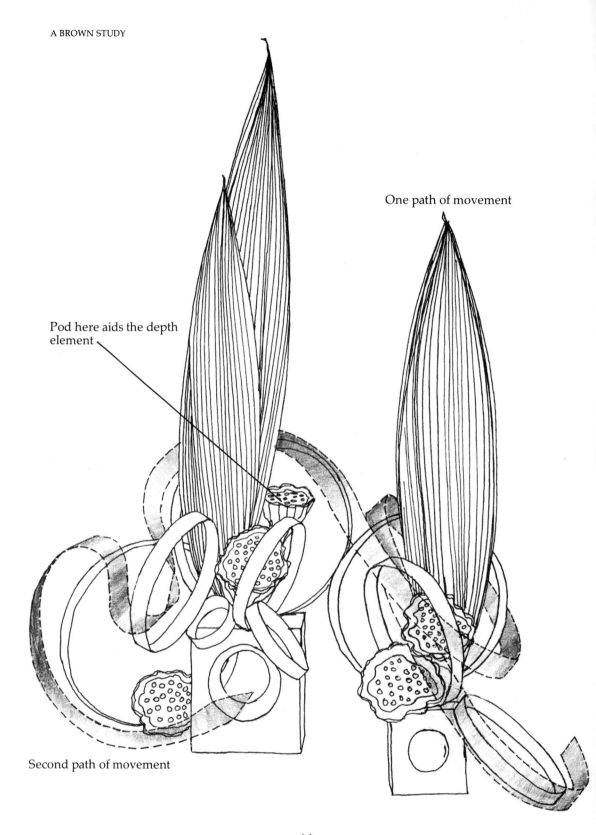

One path of movement

Pod here aids the depth element

Second path of movement

64

A thin sliver of wood for support

Design Analysis

The three leaves make a strong vertical framework that is bold, definite and dignified. For contrast the circles create a lighter and more buoyant rhythm and tie together the two separate groupings, and give the design further dimension.

There is a pleasing proportion of space and solids in plant material and containers – space and solids balance each other.

The visual weight of the leaves is offset by the spaces in the structure of the arrangement and those involving the containers. The seedheads also play their part in the balance and relate in rhythm to the circular movement of the outline.

There are three main textures, the ribbed surface of the leaves, pitted, rough lotus pods, and smooth, matt wood strips and containers.

Background colour relates to the monochromatic scheme, and gives added depth to the space element. Experimenting with different colours behind arrangements of this kind demonstrates the effect of the background on the voids and character of the design. Tan, green and mustard were tried for effect here, and whilst all three enhanced the spaces of the design, they tended to subdue the impact of the line and form of the leaves. The brown intensifies their qualities.

Technical details

Leaves were anchored in dry foam, inserted into the containers. The circles rest on the rim of the vases or against the sides stabilised with a minute blob of sticky plasticine.

The leaves were given extra support by a thin piece of bark glued to the lower section.

15
Grey Ghosts

Although the colour content of this dried arrangement is neutral and subdued, a distinctive range of form and texture provides considerable visual interest. Once assembled, it is a design that can be varied with other attractive substitutes.

The banksia flowers, for instance, could be replaced by other sculptural, dried items like fir cones, poppy seedheads, dried protea flowers or calyxes, sunflower seedheads, to name just a few possibilities. Again, a few fresh flowers like chrysanthemums, dahlias or roses would add a stronger colour contrast. Shiny red peppers, aubergines or apples would give a dramatic contrast of texture as well as colour, and so would leaves with autumn tints. Pinky-grey succulents would blend rather than contrast for a quieter harmony – there are so many effects to experiment with.

The attractive filigree-like pattern of the opuntia (prickly pear) can be used to promote a subtle see-through effect. The colour of the background will, for the same reason, play a lively part in the design itself and influence its character, as can be appreciated in the comparison of the dark grey and the red backgrounds used here.

I found the prickly pear in Malta and it had skeletonised itself naturally on the plant. An alternative for a similar effect would be sea-fern or skeletonised magnolia leaves.

The banksia flowers of Australian origin, are a souvenir of a flower festival at Durham cathedral many years ago. They are amazingly tough and durable

and I have toyed with the idea now and again of spraying them with colour, but felt it might detract from their distinctive shape and texture. The quaint grey seed-pods are from Pretoria in South Africa.

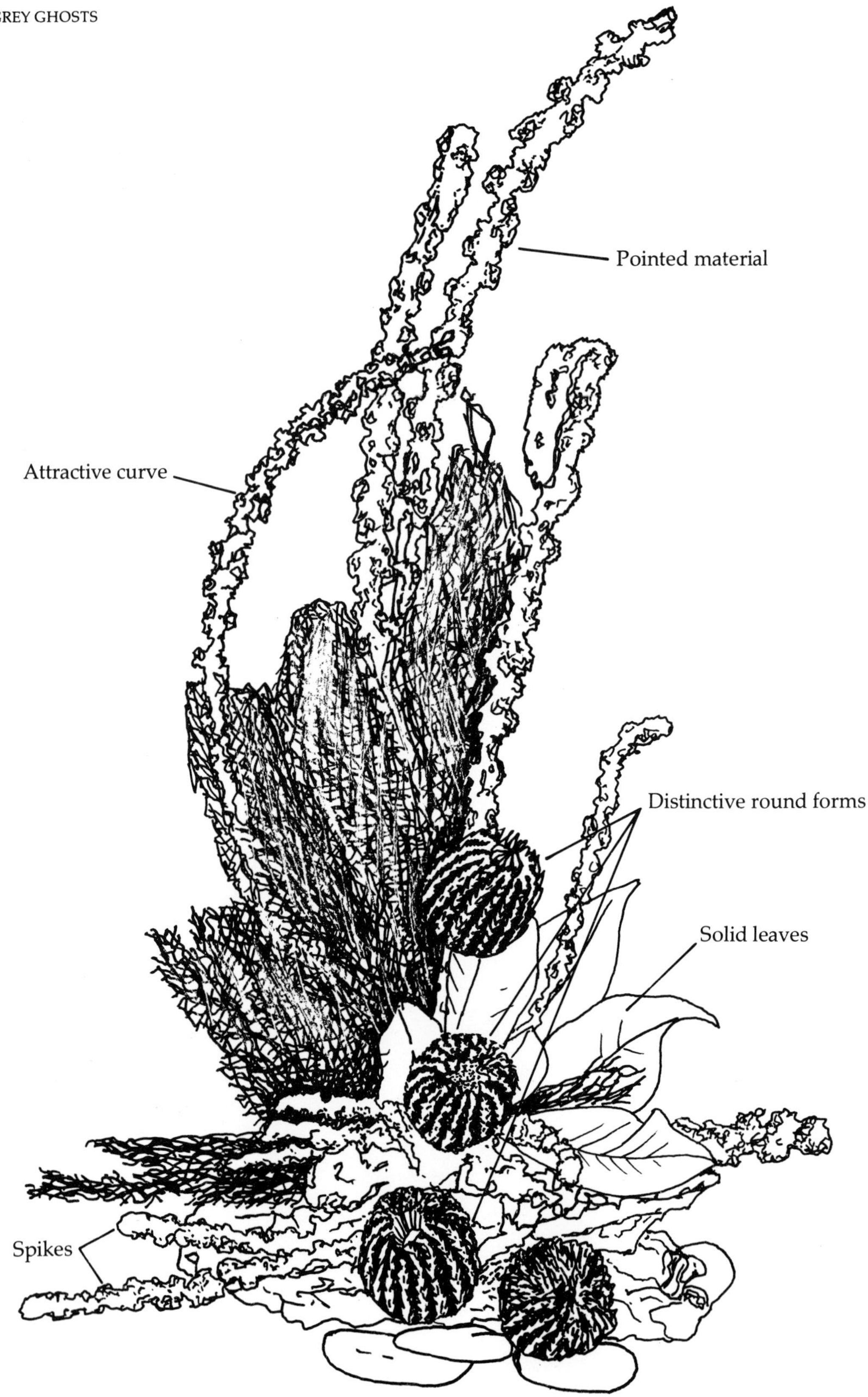

Pointed material

Attractive curve

Distinctive round forms

Solid leaves

Spikes

Technical Detail

Stems inserted into dry floral foam which fits into recesses in the container. When fresh material and water is added dip the dried stem ends in melted wax or coat with varnish to protect from damp. Small, flat strips of wood were glued at the base of each piece of opuntia for easy anchorage to the foam. (I find that 'ice lolly' sticks are ideal for this!)

Design Analysis

The surface qualities of the various plants can be analysed in terms of their harmony and contrast.

The opuntia has a rough surface, which could also be described as lacey.

Verbascum spikes are woolly, matt and downy.

The banksia flowers are rough and hairy. Magnolia leaves supply the contrast of smooth, matt surfaces, and the grey seedpods are smooth, and slightly downy. The container is also matt.

Predominant sensation of the design therefore is of roughness of textures, with minor contrasts. There is again variety and contrast of form, with pointed, round and transitional shapes.

The pattern of the arrangement is conventional with a rhythmic sequence from the heavier items at the centre to the lighter at the outline. The line of the verbascum spikes adds a buoyant quality, and the spaces created are a contrast to the more solid forms. As there is considerable variety of the elements, texture, form and colour is grouped for a smoother sequence and unified presentation.

I made the container from plastic clay (needs no firing) with wire netting as strengthener. It is coloured with a blend of art powder paints, and the dried magnolia leaves were given a very light coating of the mixture also.

Close-up of seed pod

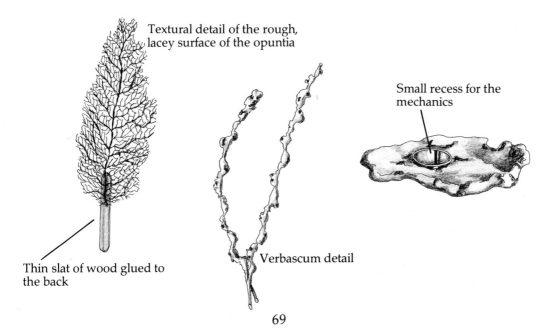

Textural detail of the rough, lacey surface of the opuntia

Small recess for the mechanics

Thin slat of wood glued to the back

Verbascum detail

69

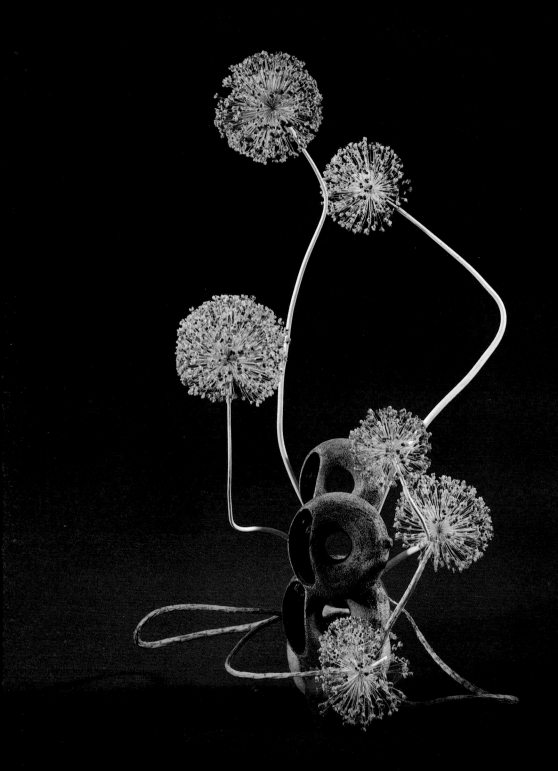

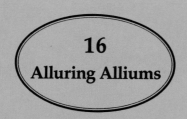

16
Alluring Alliums

There is something very satisfying about a compact round shape, especially when this is further embellished with colour, or a distinctive texture.

Alliums are greatly favoured by flower arrangers as they are decorative and useful both as fresh plants, and when dried.

There are many kinds, some growing wild, and the garden varieties are easy to cultivate. *Allium giganteum* used here has deep lilac orbs of colour in early summer, followed by seedheads, that are very attractive when green, and again when they are dried.

These sculptural rounded forms have great design attributes and can be used to create interesting effects mixed with other forms, or used alone, when their lovely structures can be fully appreciated.

On this occasion they are combined with curving stems to make a lively pattern that has a jaunty, buoyant rhythm. The design was planned to accentuate the roundness of the forms. But to avoid a static look, it was necessary to isolate each form in space, and to achieve this I confess I had to cheat a little. Originally, the allium heads were on quite straight stems, which would have been ideal for a tall arrangement with a vertical line exploited, but as this did not suit this particular design concept the line had to be altered and the heads were cut off (I am sorry about that, it sounds rather brutal) and re-inserted into hollow stems with a more wayward line. Since these belong to a near relative (wild alliums found in Cornwall) I do not feel too guilty over the surgery performed in the interest of the design. These stems have a most distinctive colour, having dried naturally to a pleasing milky-white.

The container choice was important to the sculptural aspect of the arrangement, and to suit its format I tampered a little with the vase as well. Clive Brooker designed it in a horizontal line, but by placing it vertically it becomes more fully integrated into the rhythm and pattern of the composition and as part of the overall structure ceases to function just as a vase.

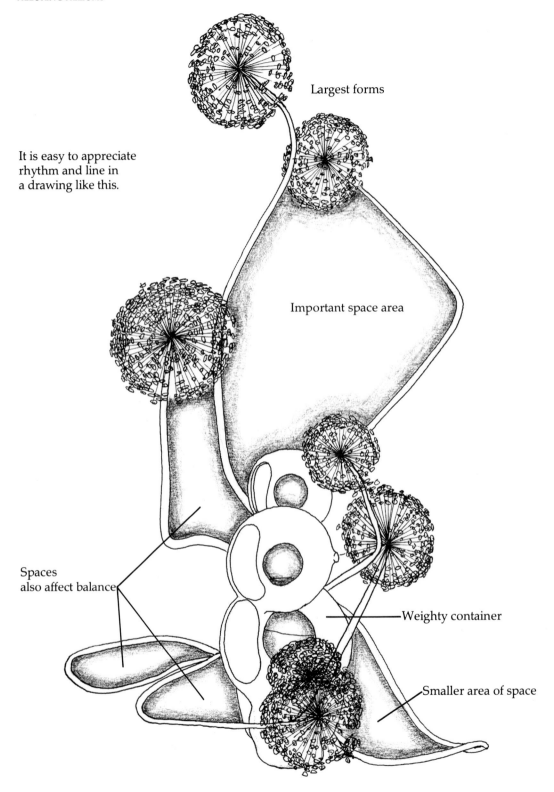

Largest forms

It is easy to appreciate
rhythm and line in
a drawing like this.

Important space area

Spaces
also affect balance

Weighty container

Smaller area of space

72

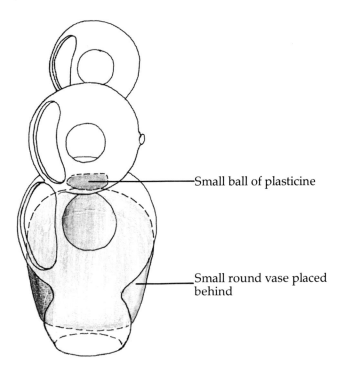

Small ball of plasticine

Small round vase placed behind

Design Analysis

As the design is a play on round forms, everything used should contribute to this aspect.

The roundness of the alliums, is emphasised by the pattern of the container, and the line of the design carries the eye in a circular rhythm –nothing interferes with the flow of movement.

As well as compact form, the alliums have a most attractive texture. This roughness is repeated in the gritty surface of the vase for further harmony. The smoothness of the matt stems and the openings in the container give some contrast.

Colours are mellow with a background that harmonises, but being of darker value gives depth to the space areas, and stronger emphasis to line and texture. Balance is interesting, with the three larger and visually heavier spheres at the top of the design to counter the force of

the container. The spaces created here (see diagram) have considerable visual weight also. Again, the space areas on the left hand side, balance the extra spheres on the right. It is a balance of solid and space throughout, repeated finally in the pattern of the vase.

Rhythm is vigorous, but since the areas of interest are distributed throughout the arrangement with no fixed or over-dominant emphasis at any one point, the eye is drawn smoothly through the entire design, and can start its journey anywhere.

Illustrations

It was important to keep the holding device as unobtrusive as possible. The stems are held in a ball of plasticine (potter's clay will also suit) resting on the second round container placed to the back of the other.

73

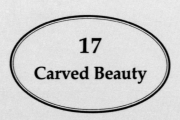

17
Carved Beauty

An interpretation with dried material to complement the figurine, a slender and elegant lady from Zimbabwe, carved from the wood of the jacaranda tree. Texture is satin-smooth and the colour a beautiful creamy white.

These fabulous trees were in bloom when I visited Rhodesia (as it then was) and their heavenly lilac-blue was quite breathtaking. Now I have a permanent reminder of this land of sunshine, colourful birds, and brilliant flowers, and above all, of the splendid flower arrangers I met there in very troubled circumstances.

It is a most enriching experience to meet the flower arrangers of other countries, both for the artistic benefit and also the close bonds of friendship which develop, and my Rhodesian trip was memorable on both counts.

The visiting flower arranger is often presented with special objects or products of the country, that can become a source of inspiration later. With attractive accessories like my figurine it is easy to create a theme. As with any accessory, the main designing aim is to capture and portray its special features with harmonious plant material in a suitable presentation. The figure here has a fairly representational aspect, but the line is exaggerated and much of the detail is omitted. The style of the arrangement is therefore adapted to suit these characteristics.

The distinctive sculptural and tactile qualities of this figurine prompted the choice of plant material with a close relationship, so that accessory and material have a true affinity and one promotes the other. The outline, and the wooden flowers also have a carved and moulded quality.

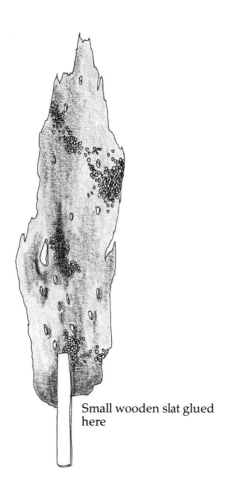

Small wooden slat glued here

Design Analysis

To stress the slender, sculptural line of the figurine, the design had to be tall and elegant. The bleached opuntia gives a moulded and rather ethereal background, and forms the ascending line of the design.

To avoid visual heaviness and too solid a structure, and to strengthen the sculptural effect of the arrangement, the rest of the outline is a curving line – with fronds of dried palm to add rhythm and space, and direct attention to the centre of the design and the figure.

Balance, proportion and scale are adapted to the dimensions of the figurine.

The accent at the base gives the necessary visual weight without detracting from the line of the figure.

There are distinctive textures, with the smoothness of the wood contrasted by the rougher, lacy surface of the opuntia. The palm fronds have a compatible woody texture supported by the seedheads and made-up flowers. These are smooth inside to complement the wood.

There is repetition of various forms throughout the design to tie together accessory and plant material. The 'flowers' also look like carvings. Colours are strongly unified with the light cream of flowers, palm, opuntia and wood base repeating the blond wood. There are touches of brown and beige for a slight contrast.

Technical Details

The opuntia and palm are held in dry plastic foam on a small holder anchored to the wooden base. Small slats of wood glued to the ends of the opuntia make it easier to anchor these safely.

The flowers are made of pointed seedpods wired around the stalk of the eucalyptus seedheads and covered with brown gutta-percha.

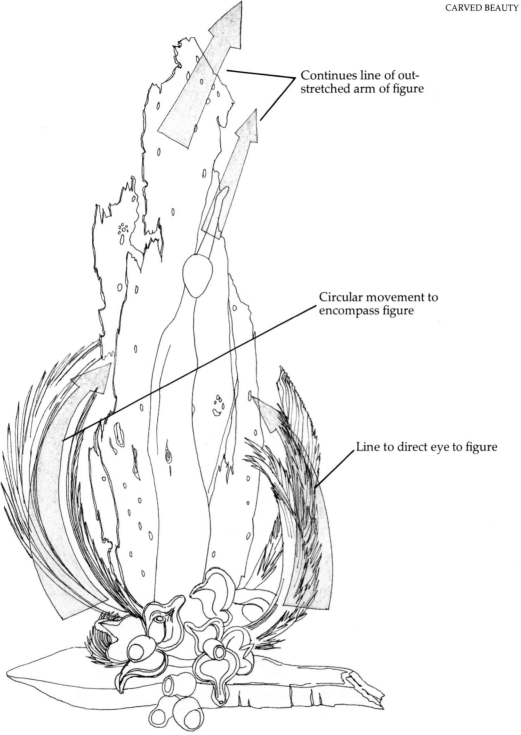

Continues line of out-
stretched arm of figure

Circular movement to
encompass figure

Line to direct eye to figure

Diagram to illustrate how the line and form of the figurine is given full emphasis by the nature
and organisation of the plant material.

18
Treasures

Another arrangement based on plant material collected from different parts of the world, this time with entirely natural curios.

Flower arrangers holiday mementoes tend not to be of the gift shop variety, as even 'off-duty', the natural instinct for collecting soon asserts itself when eager eyes survey the new terrain and its potential.

I think my husband took me to the remote little island off the coast of Tunisia on the very edge of the desert in the hope there was nothing to collect for flower arranging, and we could travel home, for once, with a respectable amount of baggage.

Alas, I could not resist the palms in their embryonic wonder. There were scores of them lying around in the sand around the base of the date palms, which apart from olives, were the only trees of any significance on the island. I knew instinctively that their fascinating structure and great diversity of line would be an inspiration later.

The bamboo husks from Kenya are totally different in character but no less distinctive in colour, form and texture. The surfaces are satin-smooth as though carved from ivory. They came from a plant of quite substantial proportions and are the husks that were attached to the main stalk. In the arrangement the sharp pointed tip is placed downwards to display the curve and sheen to full advantage. I spent two very happy weeks in Kenya with the Nairobi flower club, and found great inspiration in their plant material, and 'taka-taka', (bits and pieces to us). That was a few years ago now, but the 'taka-taka' as you see, is still intact.

Complementing the creamy colour of the husks are quaintly shaped gourds (calabash) from South Africa. Their smooth, suave shapes have the same appeal as sea worn shells and pebbles and each one is fashioned differently.

The design was finalised with the rounded forms of the impressive king protea calyxes. Here though they look more like beautiful wood carvings and, I think I prefer proteas in this form anyway.

Sculptural form

An interesting piece of palm

Exciting shapes

Second placement

Design Analysis

Form: This is bold and sculptural throughout. There is enough contrast without the variety of shapes being over-subscribed. The round and solid form of the gourds are a suitably strong contrast to the free form shapes of the embryo palm.

Line: Dramatic movement is created by the palm fronds, repeated in the line of the gourds.

Textures: The embryo palm is rough and prickly, bamboo husks smooth and silky, proteas are smooth on the inside, slightly downy on the outside. Gourds are smooth and semi-shiny. Containers (not very visible) are partly rough, partly smooth.

Colour: Light and dark values keep the design from becoming visually heavy and static. Brown and cream is a very satisfying colour harmony.

Balance: The longer line of the palm is balanced by the second placement and the greater number of husks distributed to the right.

In assembling: The units are grouped for greater harmony and a unified structure. Though assembled in a fairly conventional pattern, line, form, colour and space are organised in a dramatic sequence. Palm and gourds create important areas of space in their line and placement.

Technical Details

The palm fronds were quite heavy to anchor and since the material need not be in water, it was easier to use a lump of clay. It is wedged into the opening of the vase, with the bulk sitting on top.

The second smaller container is almost hidden, but it is effective in raising the palm frond and displaying it to greater advantage.

Close-up of each object which further illustrates their special characteristics and contrasts

19

'And The Birds Sang
Their Evening Prayer'
(Kiekegaard)

An interpretative landscape type arrangement, where a naturalistic theme is built around driftwood bird forms, which are entirely as I found them by the loch in Scotland. Shape and gesture which is incredibly bird-like, pointing earnestly to the sky above gave me the strong impression of someone totally involved in Godly conversation.

The natural setting and mood is further promoted with stones, succulents, tufts of *Stachys lanata,* rue, atriplex seed-heads and flax. The scenic background adds further atmosphere to the theme.

Landscape arrangements are perhaps the most well-loved of designs for nature herself is always enchanting in her endless moods, effects, and aspects, and for the flower arranger, and artists everywhere, the most faithful source of inspiration.

I came across the quotation in *The Countryman,* in an article by Sir Herbert Read, and being a country woman, felt impelled to attempt an interpretation. Words have great power to inspire, and I made a note of two other poetic descriptions in the same article. 'A tender desolation of purple and russet tints.' 'A trickle of bog water in a ferny rill'.

Interpretations with romantic connotations appeal emotionally, and imaginative titles offered to the competitor at flower shows, are more likely to elevate the imaginative content of the themes portrayed. It is easy to respond to evocative titles borrowed from the poets such as
'Green thoughts in a green glade'. (Richard Church)
'Amid the smiles and tears of tender spring'. (Edith Holden)
'Plants which love the moisture and the shade'. (Southey)
'When night is on the hills'. (Herbert Trench)
'A tremulous splendour in the autumn dew'. (Alexander Smith)
To capture the magic of these words in an interpretation with plant material is quite a challenge, but a pleasant one.

I enjoyed the effort here, thanks to nature providing me with such delightful accessories, and the poet for his inspirational words.

Aims of Interpretative Design

In this style of arranging, the main objective is to capture the atmosphere and mood of the theme, whether telling a story, stating a philosophy, or expressing a mood, emotion or idea. It is a very stimulating area of designing, which involves using the imagination to communicate the interpretation to the viewer, or the judge on competitive occasions.

There is an abundant range of subjects which can be depicted and the style can vary from naturalistic to abstract. But whatever the choice of presentation, everything used should work for the portrayal of the title. Colour, shape, line, textures and character of the plant material should promote the theme, aided by the accessories or background effects if these improve and strengthen the interpretation.

This is a landscape type design which aims at conveying a scene from nature – a quiet corner of the garden or the country-side in the evening light. Plant material is not exotic but chosen to suit the accessories and outdoor aspect. The accessories of natural wood (and therefore plant material) are the feature of the design and carry the interpretation. Background adds interest without being too distracting.

The main temptation in interpretative work is overstatement and being too literal. Something left to the imagination of the viewer is recommended, and a little subtlety is often more effective than the very obvious. Too many man-made accessories can also detract from the importance of the plant material and very often the expressiveness of this alone is powerful enough to tell the story.

Technique

Landscape arrangements can be enhanced with sense of depth to suggest a larger panorama. The scale and placement of the units can influence this aspect.

Larger items like branches, driftwood or large pieces of bark can interpret the taller features in a landscape, with smaller sized material like flowers or small accessories as contrast. Leaves, stones and shells placed in between can create transitional depth and add to the scenic effect.

There are three separate placements here to give the illusion of depth, through a foreground, middle area, and a background.

The *actual* background placed behind the composition adds another dimension.

Diagram to show the depth and height relationship of the composition

84

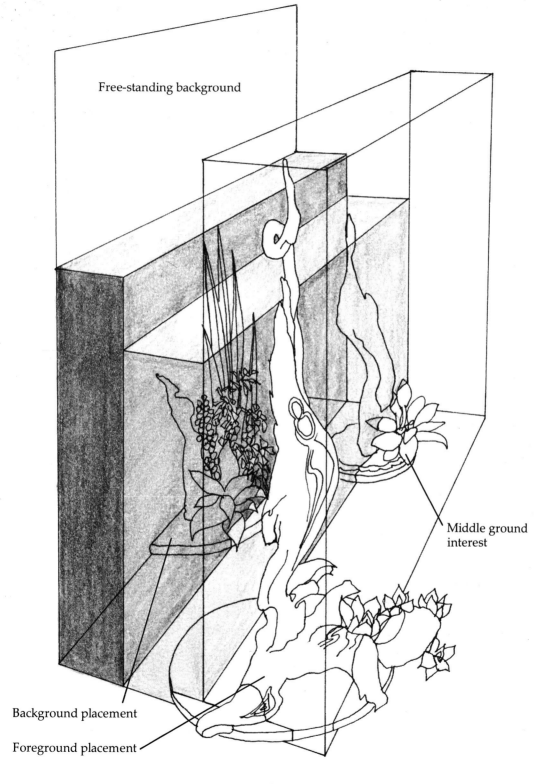

Free-standing background

Middle ground
interest

Background placement

Foreground placement

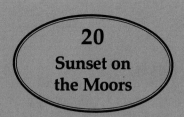

20
Sunset on the Moors

Another interpretative landscape type design using very simple plant material and accessories – the kind that could easily be picked up on a walk on the moor and hills (and what flower arranger comes back empty-handed from these expeditions?).

The gorse branch, for instance, is a common enough feature of the countryside. Admittedly it has to be the right shape and calibre, some are definitely collector's pieces, and more special than others. The one used here is rather bold and dramatic, as might be expected from the wild and desolate terrain of Dartmoor in Devon. With a little help of a friend of like mind and inclination I found several fine specimens, that were charred, bent and twisted by the elements. We were returning from judging at a flower show, and dressed of course in our smart clothes!

The accessories to complement the branch, are also natural objects, that fit in with the theme – just small pieces of charred wood that look amazingly like grouse and other moorland birds (yes, I am a birdwatcher too!).

The sprigs of heather did, in fact, come from the garden, but where it abounds by the acre, a small bunch would not be missed or the countryside despoiled. Lichened stones, heather, roots, or dried twigs bleached by the sun and rain, and that lovely grey moss, or sprigs of wild thyme, are also worth looking for. As for the gorse, no farmer would lament its disappearance and might even appreciate the cleaning up operation of flower arrangers. I can, to date, lay claim for tidying up parts of the Yorkshire Moors, Dartmoor, and the clifftops at Land's End and all of Wales where gorse is very rampant. Resourceful flower arrangers travel with an old pair of gardening gloves, hack-saw and dungarees in the boot of the car, and so are well equipped to collect the awkward or the unexpected treasure.

It may sound arduous but so often it is the special oddities we gather that add appeal. With a little imagination, and a keen collector's instinct, much can be achieved with little.

Design Comments

Choice of plant material, and a suitable setting, are the two aspects that promote the theme.

The powerful line and structure of the bare, blackened branch symbolises ruggedness, bleakness and the force of the elements. Sparsity of additional plant material supports these impressions.

The sunset colours of the background add meaning and atmosphere, whilst the accessories help to further the interpretation – the scene implied is easy to imagine.

The line of the branch and its dimensions also suggest height and distance, with the contrast of the low placement of the heather to increase the illusion. The accessories placed on different levels also add to the depth element of the design, and so do the space areas organised throughout. Placements therefore help to create a foreground, middle and background of interest – a typical feature of landscape arrangements already discussed in the previous arrangement.

Advancing and receding colours are organised to play their part in the rhythm and depth of the design, especially in the strong contrast of red and black.

The repetition of colour in the outline of the arrangement and base maintains continuity and flow for design unity. The scale and proportion suggested by components of different sizes help to convey the larger panorama in nature.

Technical Details

Though appearing as one, there are three separate placements here to create the landscape effect.

The branch is top-heavy, and so was firmly anchored with black plasticine on a strong pinholder. To aid this operation two thin slats of wood were secured to the branch at both sides with black insulating tape, with a few inches extending beyond to slide into the mechanics.

The upright accessory of wood sits on a small lump of brown plasticine.

Two thin slats of wood secured with black sticky tape

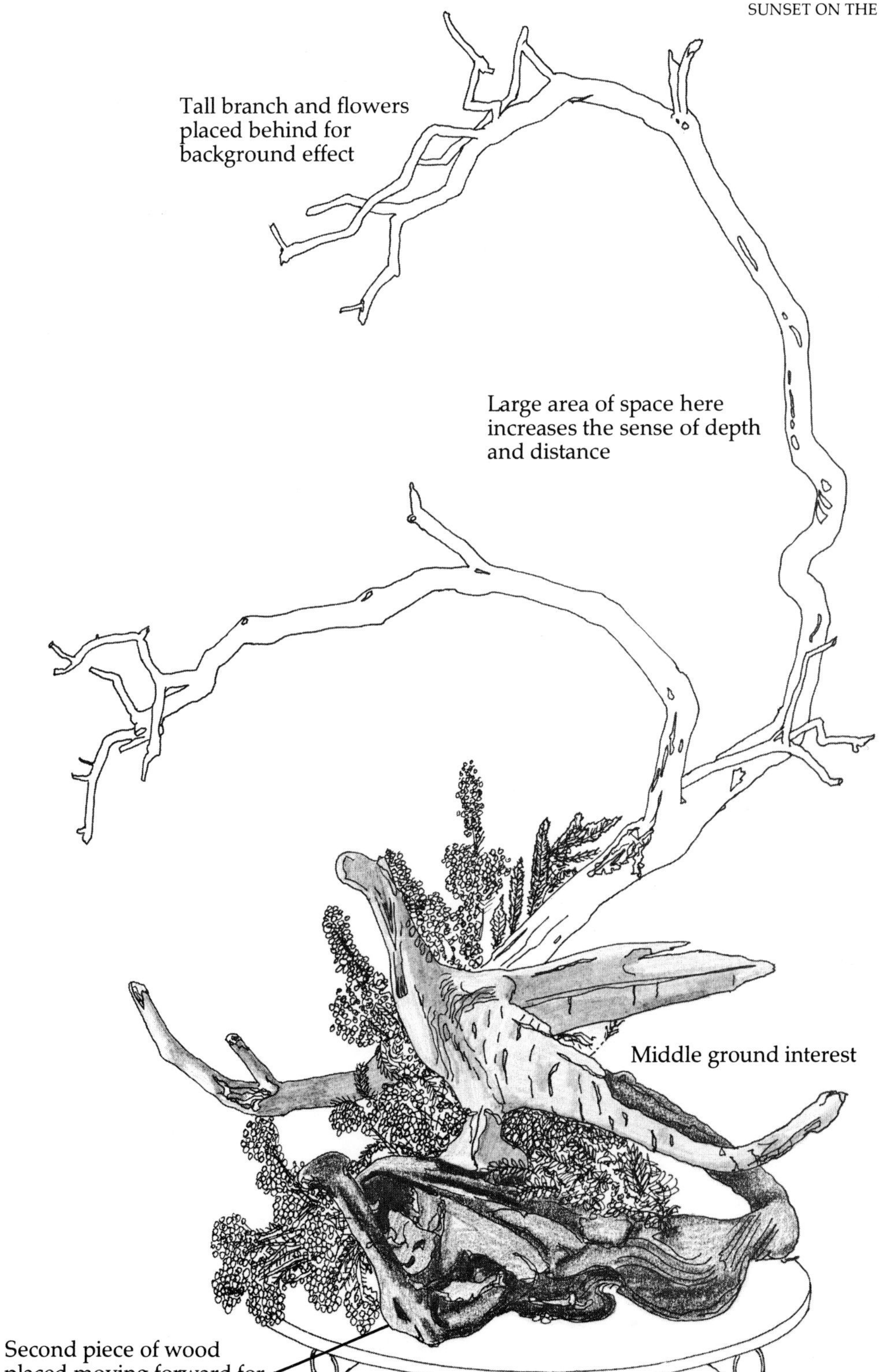

Tall branch and flowers
placed behind for
background effect

Large area of space here
increases the sense of depth
and distance

Middle ground interest

Second piece of wood
placed moving forward for
foreground interest

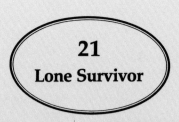

21
Lone Survivor

A theme interpreted in a design that is mainly non-naturalistic, but as there is an element of naturalism in the presentation of flower and leaf, the style is not totally abstract.

You may not think the theme is a particularly happy one, but it has imaginative possibilities, and it holds for me a certain nostalgia and personal recollections, which are incidentally, very happy and romantic rather than sad.

Inspiration is the greatest motivating factor whatever the style, and re-capturing certain moments in time is a great stimulus to the imagination, and an easy way to begin an interpretive design.

This theme is built around that jagged piece of wood, which is a genuine treasure. It is part of the hulk of a ship sunk off the Cornish coast beneath the waves for doubtless many years, judging by its rusty barnacle-encrusted surface and eroded structure. I stayed in a house overlooking a beautiful cove with a flower arranger wholly compatible to myself in searching for the unusual. Naturally she knew about the wreck, and how the occasional remnant emerged when the tide was out. Alas, during my stay, this occurred around 3.00 am, and, in late October, the prospect of wading up the creek at that strange hour daunted even the likes of me. But, with the generosity so typical of flower arrangers everywhere, she parted with a few from her own collection. It was better than winning the pools, as money cannot buy such strange and beautiful oddities and the most avid beachcomber seldom finds such distinctive structures.

Now, many tides later, here I am deep in recollection, and re-inspired. It is easy to imagine a storm at sea, with raging skies and perilous waters as in a Turner painting. With plant material we are a little more restricted than the painter is with his canvas. But experiences enjoyed can flame enthusiasm, and impressions drawn from memory can be coloured by the imagination – to become more vivid and enhanced expressions.

Design Analysis

The expressiveness of the design is promoted through placements and choice of elements.

The driftwood hulk, elevated and poised on the rim of the container, creates the appropriate atmosphere suggesting disaster and danger.

The line and directional movement of the contorted hazel twigs support the implication by adding extra turbulence.

The placement of the fatsia leaf adds to the dimension of depth and distance – an illusion supported by the background which recedes. This also adds atmosphere

Lower section of rusty iron

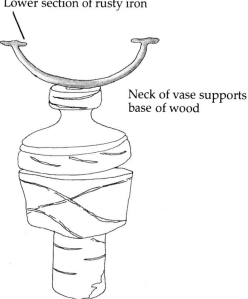

Neck of vase supports base of wood

through its sombre, murky, textured surface.

The contrast of the fresh and living, and perishable with the more enduring, stresses the fragile, vulnerable aspect of human life exposed to the harsh elements. An implication all the more convincing with just a single, lonely bloom.

The combination of fresh and dried also adds to design interest, with the texture of the leaf a strong contrast to the rough, gritty surface of the wood. The smooth, matt surface of the flower also enhances this aspect of the design and the fresh material adds colour contrast.

Balance is carefully organised for interpretative impact, but at the same time to preserve the visual stability of the design. The flower, leaf and enclosed space on the left adjust the pull of the longer and more powerful line of the wood on the right – without over-compensating (see diagram).

The rhythm of the design is vigorous and varied.

Technical Details

There are sections of the original iron foundation still left in the wood, and the two at the base in the back sit neatly on the edge of the vase.

Across this was placed a flat slat of thin wood to support a small well-pinholder for the plant material.

Background is wide studio paper (the kind used in photography) painted with powder paints to suggest a stormy sky.

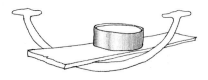

A small well-pinholder rests on a small piece of wood across the metal bar

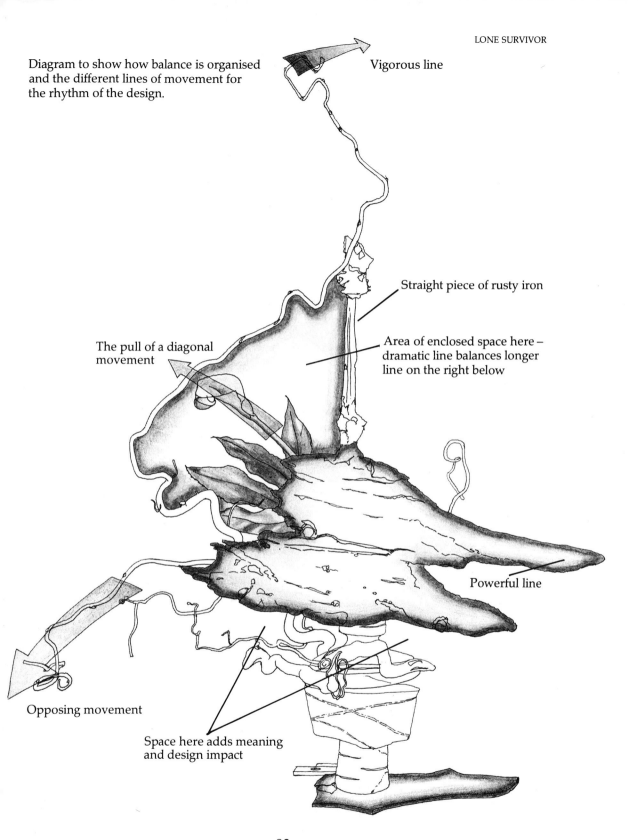

Diagram to show how balance is organised and the different lines of movement for the rhythm of the design.

Vigorous line

Straight piece of rusty iron

The pull of a diagonal movement

Area of enclosed space here – dramatic line balances longer line on the right below

Powerful line

Opposing movement

Space here adds meaning and design impact

93

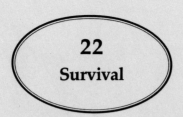

22
Survival

The same piece of wood and vase and a similar subject interpreted, but an aspect drawn from the subject is now presented in a more abstract style. It is a simplified version of the theme, with most of the detail removed to make a direct statement.

The previous design was sparse and stark, but this is stripped of all except essentials, and there is nothing left that is superfluous. The interpretation therefore relies on design strength to put across the theme effectively.

Compared to the other arrangement where the flower, combined with greenery was fairly naturalistically presented, the tulips here are just two lines with points of colour moving in a strong diagonal direction to support the angle of the driftwood. The natural association of the flowers in unimportant and subordinated to the requirements of the design.

By eliminating some of the plant material and effects, the force of line, form and texture is more assertive, as they are now more sharply defined. Without distracting detail, the abstract qualities inherent in the material does all the work and what is lost in decorative effect is gained through the power of simplicity.

It is not necessarily a better interpretation or design structure than the previous example. It is included for comparison, with approach and presentation adapted to another aspect of the theme.

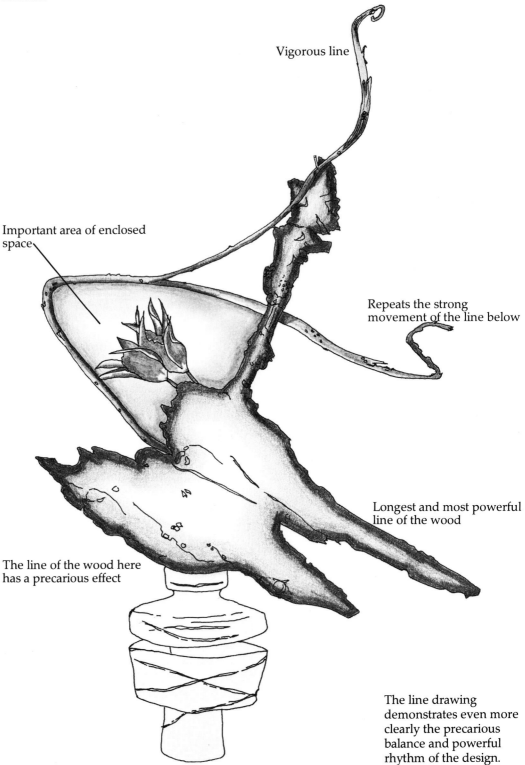

Vigorous line

Important area of enclosed space

Repeats the strong movement of the line below

Longest and most powerful line of the wood

The line of the wood here has a precarious effect

The line drawing demonstrates even more clearly the precarious balance and powerful rhythm of the design.

Design Analysis

Though there is a minimum of plant material, the strong, expressive quality of each item works for the interpretation.

If we compare again the two designs, the different angle of each placement can be appreciated. The line of the driftwood here is more acutely diagonal and precarious, and so generates an even greater sense of instability and peril.

The powerful movement created by the setsuka branch intensifies this aspect and its implication.

The flowers increase activity with an opposing line as does the line of the container.

Space is more severely defined due to the elimination of detail. Notice how much more pronounced the space below the driftwood and the vase has become without the transitional branches.

Space is also a more powerful element seen against the plain background with every area getting maximum display.

Repetition of form and space to create the rhythmic sequence of the design is also more evident a feature, and textures are more noticeable.

Though the line and rhythm are exaggerated for design emphasis and interpretation, as in the previous example, the visual balance is still intact and organised along similar lines, with the pull of the flowers and enclosed space on one side of the central axis of the arrangement counterbalanced by the greater impact of the wood on the opposite side. A sense of stability that is too obvious however is avoided, and note that the base under the arrangement is now removed.

Other Details

Flowers are in glass tubes taped to the back of the wood. Lower end of branch is also attached to wood.

23
Treasures of
the Deep

A variation of the last arrangements using similar material, and
featuring again the sea-worn sculptures of the Cornish coast, this time
coupled with other trivia (or treasure?) found along the sea-shore.
The rusty wood is now complemented by swirls of sea-wrack,
fantastically moulded into sculptural shapes of dramatic quality, with
flowers and succulents that add colour and further interest.
This is more colourful and visually richer than the previous
compositions to suggest an underwater medley of life and colour, and
is more pictorial in content.
Themes built around the sea and shore have imaginative appeal and
are always very popular at flower show competitions. Out come the
shells and stones, coral, sea-fern, cork floats and bits of net and lobster
pots, and many other bewitching objects.
Beachcombing is a fascinating occupation indulged in by young and
old, but the flower arranger's approach is coloured by the need to find
the more unusual – something that will make a stunning contribution to
titles like 'Underwater fantasy', 'Full fathom five', 'Wonders of the deep',
'Beachcomber', 'Seascape', or quotations such as 'In the depth of the
purple sea.'
With a rich profusion of flotsam and jetsam however it is easy to over-
accentuate the interest and detail. Many a marine theme lovingly
executed is judged as having 'too many accessories'. It must be
remembered that in competitive show exhibits, stones, shells and
anything other than plant material is an accessory, and restraint
is needed for the plants to predominate and to tell the story, with
the other objects to highlight but not to overpower. Again, with a
rich variety of texture, shapes and colour, care must be exercised
in the choice of background. The effectiveness of a few distinctive
elements which interpret the theme eloquently can be ruined
by a lurid background which overstates with bright blue skies
and clouds and seagulls.

Design Comments

The chosen elements of texture, colour, space and line promote the style and atmosphere of this interpretation.

Texture. There is harmony and contrast of surface qualities. These are predominantly rough, coarse, rusty and gritty, displayed in wood, metal, sea-wrack and flowers. Contrast is effected through the smooth succulents and matt, plain background, which is a suitable foil for the eye-catching textures.

Colour. There is enough variety for the interpretation and design interest without an excessive number of contrasts. The beautiful scarlet nerines give a glow and vibrancy set off by the colour of wood and metal and grey-blue succulents. Background colour is not over-dominant. The touches of white in the sea-wrack adds an attractive highlight.

Space. The voids created enhance the overall effect with background colour brought into the structure of the design. This is of enormous benefit to rhythm, depth and beauty and also aids interpretation. The enclosed space made by the sea-wrack at the top of the arrangement, modifies the hard line of the metal supporting the vertical piece of wood.

Line. The sea-wrack gives the design an interesting and lively rhythm, and unites the elements in a pleasing line of movement. The outline it creates also makes a flattering framework for the flowers.

Balance. The organisation of all the elements discussed affects the overall balance, which is dynamic and interesting.

Sea-wrack or sea-weed is classified in the National Association's *Handbook of Schedule Definitions for Flower Arrangement* as natural plant material, so the only accessory here is the metal.

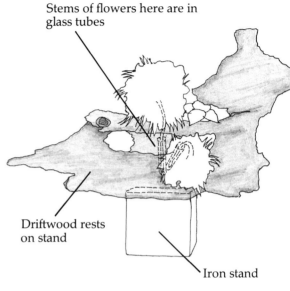

Stems of flowers here are in glass tubes

Driftwood rests on stand

Iron stand

Technical Details

Strong mechanics are necessary here as the material used is weighty.

There are two separate wood structures. The one at the back is attached to a large angular piece of rusty iron. This is almost free-standing, but for added safety the end of the wood was wedged into a cylinder made of iron. The horizontal wood in the front rests on a small but sturdy stand of iron. A small well-pinholder holds water for the three flowers above the second structure. The other two in the foreground are in glass tubes hidden by the sea-weed.

100

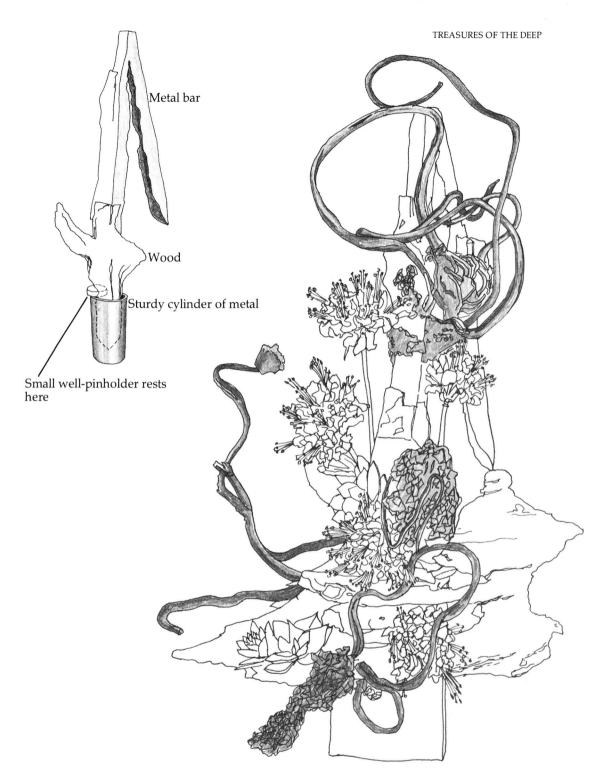

Metal bar

Wood

Sturdy cylinder of metal

Small well-pinholder rests here

The drawing illustrates the lively rhythm created by the sea-wrack supported by the silhouette of the wood

24
Grief

The keen designer appreciates the force and quality of different plant material as symbols for expression, and a close study of character and attributes can foster a deeper understanding of each plant's potential, which is a guide to the right selection for interpretation.

The distinctive or predominant quality of a plant evokes different responses. We do not have the same reaction to jagged thorns, a massive branch, or fragile flower; they are each expressive in their different, individual way, and symbolic of quite different qualities and images. The material used here, for instance is an interesting example, as the theme of the interpretation was inspired by the line, form and character of the dried agave spears, which is very impressive and commanding.

Initially it was the sculptural aspect that captured my interest, and the two spears combined to make a strong and stunning sculpture. A closer look however, revealed other qualities which influenced the progress of the design, for the angles and curves displayed in the pattern now created suggested a figure bowed in grief.

I had already added the stone which is wholly compatible in colour and texture to the agave, and completes the design structure, which could have been left in that form. Now, although sculpture is still the main feature, the flowers and leaves have added another dimension of meaning and expression. There is an added incentive to speculate and to contemplate, to assess the symbolism of each unit, and how its unique expressiveness adds to the total impression and confirmation of the theme.

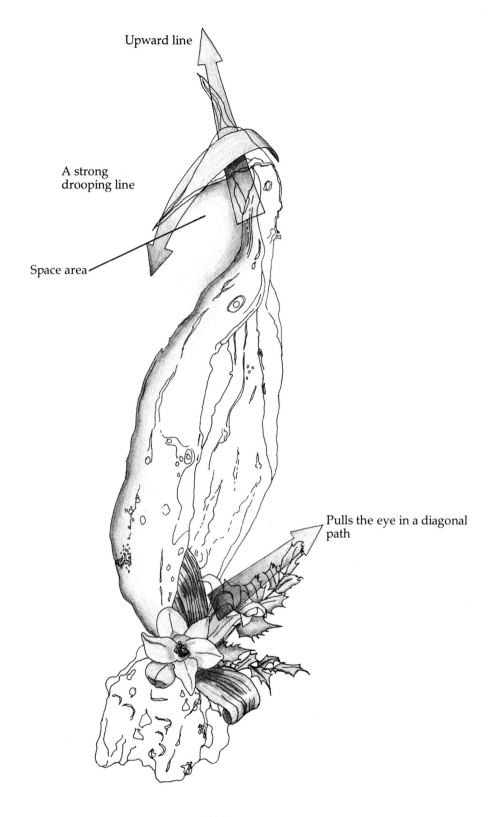

Upward line

A strong
drooping line

Space area

Pulls the eye in a diagonal
path

Design Observation

Form is strong and sculptural throughout the design – in agave spears, stones, flowers and leaves.

Textures are sharply contrasted. The agave is rough and gritty, the stones rough and pitted, and closely related in surface quality to the agave.

Mahonia (berberis) leaves are prickly. There is dramatic contrast in the smooth, satiny flowers, and semi-glossy aspidistra leaves.

The line of the spears is powerfully expressive. The larger area leads the eye upwards in a vertical movement, but the strong downward line at the left opposes this (see diagram).

The mahonia and aspidistra leaves create a secondary movement for extra design depth and definition.

The pointed lines in the petals of the flowers repeat the spikes of the agave.

Colour contrasts are sharp, background adds depth.

The space element adds to the beauty and depth of the design.

Rhythm is solemn and dignified.

Height proportion is purposely exaggerated for a stronger ascending rhythm. Stones, flowers and leaves however have substantial visual weight for balance.

The line of the mahonia leaves and that of the lilies balance the visual weight of the space area created by the downward line of the agave (see diagram).

Technique

The large, awkward shapes of the agave had to be firmly stabilised.

A flat piece of wood was glued to the inner surface of the back piece.

This was wedged into a small tin filled with clay (Polyfilla or cement will do).

The second spear sits on the stone and is anchored at the top by the groove in the first spear.

A second, smaller stone placed behind the larger one holds a small well pin-holder for the fresh material.

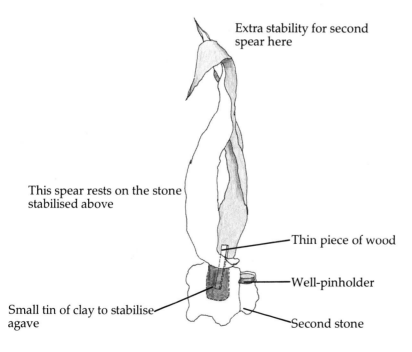

Extra stability for second spear here

This spear rests on the stone stabilised above

Thin piece of wood

Well-pinholder

Small tin of clay to stabilise agave

Second stone

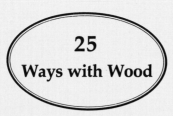

25
Ways with Wood

Most flower arrangers are driftwood collectors, and I am no exception. In fact, though I should not boast about it, I have a rather fantastic selection of this most useful and attractive commodity. Strangely though, someone else's collection always seems more impressive and desirable, which encourages one to go on searching.

Driftwood, in flower arranging terminology, includes wood from varying sources, not just what has drifted in with the tide. Indeed, the beach nowadays is rather a poor hunting ground; due no doubt to obsessive driftwood hunters, who like myself love to clean up the beaches.

Happily there are other promising sources if one is prepared to look further, even to climb the odd tree if necessary! Thick, woody branches of ivy are fairly easy to come by, and stripped of the outer bark become considerably more alluring. Wood of this nature is also in a way more versatile in use than the very heavy, or the very spectacular: it is easy to adapt line and shape to suit the purpose. Several separate pieces can be put together in varied ways to give different patterns which can be readily altered when necessary – a sort of ready-to-assemble driftwood unit, which can be juggled about to order.

The combined effect of three pieces here makes a satisfactory base for displaying a few flowers. This could easily be varied for a different line and format or more sections added to make a larger structure or a wood sculpture complete in itself.

When newly stripped of bark, ivy is very light in colour and rather dramatic and eye-catching. If a more mellow, or antique look is preferred the wood can be left outside to weather in the sun and rain to a more creamy colour. Some have even been known to soak it in water containing rusty nails or something similar for a colour change or a rougher, more rustic finish. Alternatively the smoothness of the surface could be accentuated with a wax polish, buffed to give a more sophisticated appearance, or a wood stain applied for a deeper, richer tone.

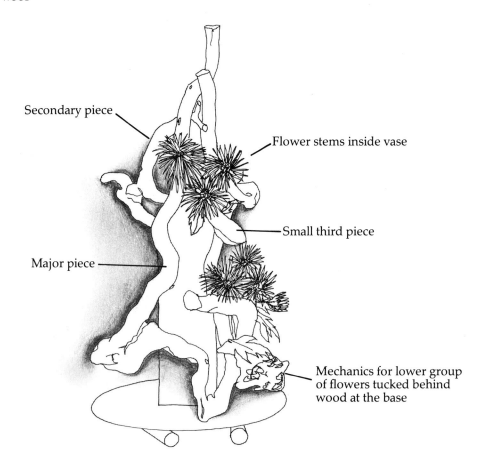

Secondary piece

Flower stems inside vase

Small third piece

Major piece

Mechanics for lower group
of flowers tucked behind
wood at the base

Design Comments

It is the wood that carries the design in
line, and pattern of space and solid. It
creates an ascending, spiralling rhythm
through its major line. Container being
vertical, supports this movement.

The base is circular, and being slightly
elevated adds further buoyancy.

There is a pleasing proportion of space
and solid created by the structural pattern,
with the additional plant material used as
an accent of texture and colour, rather
than to overfill the space areas.

In the line drawing you can trace the
rhythm of these areas which clearly illustrates the value of space in a design.

Balance is asymmetrical, with the
shorter, stubbier line on the left, balanced
by the longer one on the right. The pronounced curve at the top left is balanced
by the distribution of the flowers and the
space element of the arrangement (see
drawing).

Texture and colour of wood and
container harmonise, with surfaces that
are matt and 'grainy' – an interesting
texture which also has subtle colour
variations.

Technical Detail

The top flowers are in the vase. A small
tin with pinholder tucked behind the
vase on the base anchors the lower
placement.

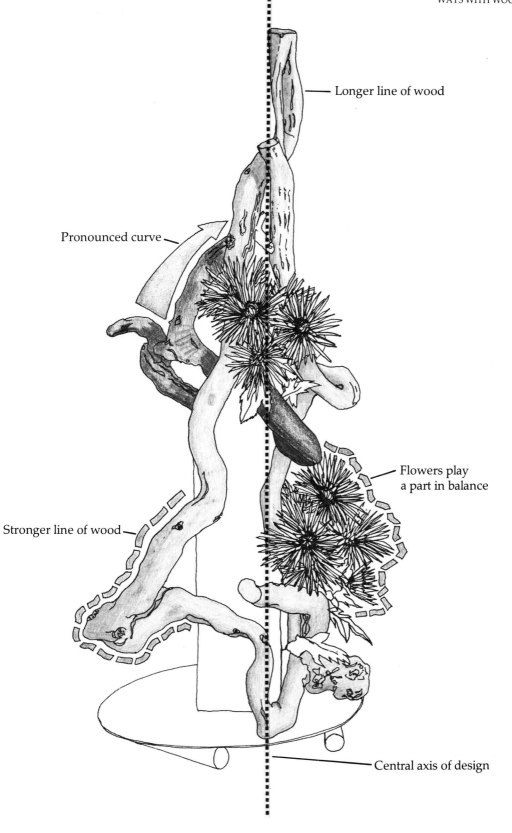

Longer line of wood

Pronounced curve

Flowers play
a part in balance

Stronger line of wood

Central axis of design

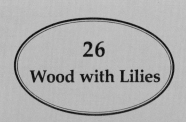

26
Wood with Lilies

Driftwood governs the basic form of this design also, with its arresting
line supported by that of dried setsuka twigs (*Salix setsuka*), the willow
with the strange fasciated branches. Combined together these inspired
the pattern of the arrangement, and established its major features.
Everything used here is rather special, for the splendour of the wood
is given added emphasis and the design a radiance with the choice of
flowers seen at varying stages of development.
A lily in my opinion has tremendous character and charisma, a queen
amongst flowers, whose elegance and dignity was surely devised for a
royal performance. Lilies invite admiration, reverence even, and add
that unmistakable touch of distinction and lustre to an arrangement,
whether mixed with other flowers or in solo appearance.
With so many varieties it is hard to single out the loveliest. There is
an astonishing range in colour alone.
The Madonna lily, so chaste and pure, is white. Regale, too is white,
but with a golden throat and deep gold anthers. For a deep warm and
dazzling yellow, there is Royal Gold, but the cooler lemon Limelight,
with a tinge of green on the outside of the petals gleams like a star.
There are other lilies in hot, sultry orange, deep apricot, and other lively
colours that give the impression of being more robust and extroverted
and showy. The sumptuous Auratum lily used here, known as the
golden rayed lily, has a golden yellow band or ray on the inner side of
the gleaming white petals speckled with reddish-brown spots. The total
effect is further enlivened by velvety chestnut anthers borne on the tips
of the slender filaments.
The driftwood is a good foil to exploit the beauty of the flowers, and
they in turn draw attention to the special features of the wood. Mutual
differences, and mutual affinity therefore benefit each other.
Discovering a happy relationship between the different units chosen
for a composition is one of the most rewarding aspects of designing,
and speaking again from a purely personal point of view, there is
something eminently satisfying about wood with lilies.

The contribution of line, form and space can
be fully appreciated in the artist's drawing

Flowers follow the
movement created by the
sweeping line of the
branches

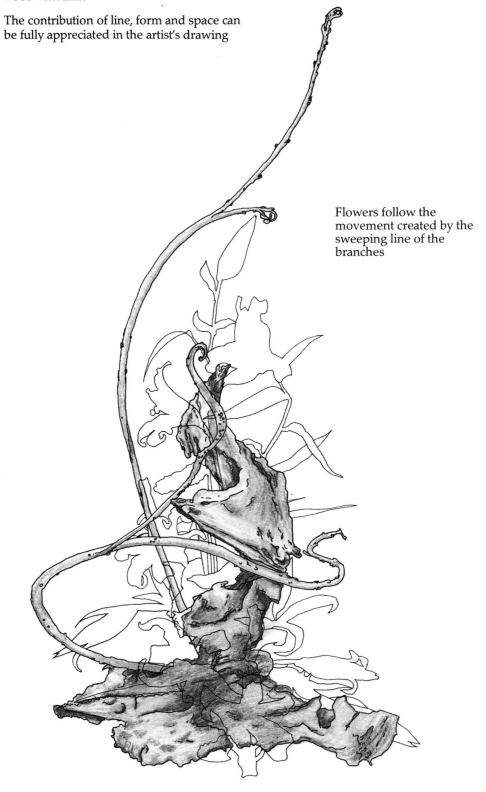

112

Design Observation

Each unit used here is dramatic and eye-catching, yet these combine well for the total effect of the design, i.e. nothing over-dominates.

The flowers match the wood in their bold, sculptural shape. The buds repeat certain shapes in the wood. Each opened bloom displaying the brown anthus and reddish brown spots has a colour that harmonises with that of the setting. The contrast of the white against brown is very pleasing.

There are some interesting textures in the design. The driftwood has a craggy, irregular, surface. This is repeated in petal formation and the raised spotted surfaces of the lilies. These textures are a contrast to the smooth waxy, qualities elsewhere in each bloom. The fasciated surfaces of the branches contribute to textural interest.

The driftwood has an arresting line, further emphasised by the line of the branches. These enliven the rhythm of the design, and also create interesting areas of space, which contrast with the solidity of the wood structure.

The space element also improves the depth of the arrangement, and helps to highlight the silhouette of the flowers it frames.

Each bloom has been carefully position-ed to face different ways so that different aspects can be seen and enjoyed, and the details emphasised. With only one type of flower used, greater variety of form is created with bud, half open and fully opened bloom.

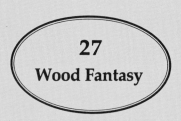

27
Wood Fantasy

This intriguing piece of wood is a slice of a hollowed tree trunk weathered by the elements to a soft creamy white, and lovely smooth texture. Its greatest asset for design, however, is its clean compact form. This I have tried to accentuate with the supporting elements, to give overall compatibility, so that whilst each object is dramatically displayed and draws attention, there is unity of purpose and presentation.
For instance, shape and space, texture and colour are harmoniously repeated throughout, so that each unit appears necessary to the total effect.
This is especially applicable to the relationship of the seed-heads and wood where the compact, sculptural shape of the solid relates convincingly to the void.
These are the outer husks that once housed bright yellow sunflowers, and later the seeds. They are now dried and sunbleached to an astonishing colour and texture, so that they look more like phantom flowers, seen only by moonlight, and in pure fantasy; flowers of the wood itself caught in silent flight.
Too fanciful? Then you might prefer a more realistic version, with the neat, round forms envisaged as clocks to symbolise time and combined with the movement of the branch, interpretive of 'A moment in time'.
To be topical though, they are unidentified flying objects – flying saucers, or other equally mysterious phenonema of extra-terrestrial origin conveyed through their placement in the design, where they do indeed seem suspended in space.
It was not easy to achieve this aspect, with the branch anchored in mid-air, but thanks to my improving skill with the electric drill, and greater ability to drive a screw in relatively straight, I achieved an effective basis for non-naturalistic presentation, with greater design flexibility. The branch is easily removed, when more naturalistic, or quite different effects are required, as seen in the design which follows.

Design Observation

This is not a naturalistic design, and placements are therefore not conventional. There is no definite central point to hold the eye, and every part of the design is an area of interest, emphasising an element which contributes to the total effect.

All the units are organised to function as though suspended in space.

A series of small dark circular bases lift the wood off the ground to give the illusion of movement. The lower placement of seed husk is raised out from the mechanics to move outwards and forwards. Anchorage of the higher placements is also well concealed to promote a similar illusion. Space is a prominent feature, which generates depth, and a three dimensional quality.

There is repetition of form in seedheads and wood, and a corresponding harmony of circular rhythm. The seedheads have their own contrasting line of movement, one forward, the other backwards. The branch leads the eye in a vertical, and again, opposing path.

Colour and form of the wood and seedhusks are similar, but there is a contrast of texture between the smoothness of the wood, and the coarser surfaces of the husks.

The branch (honeysuckle) is matt and smooth.

Background is matt, and being dark, gives greater definition to space and to the individual units.

Technical Details

Once the branch was made stable, the top seedhead was wired to it at one point and the lower seedhead is wired to a false stem inserted on to a small pinholder.

Diagram shows how the branch was made stable

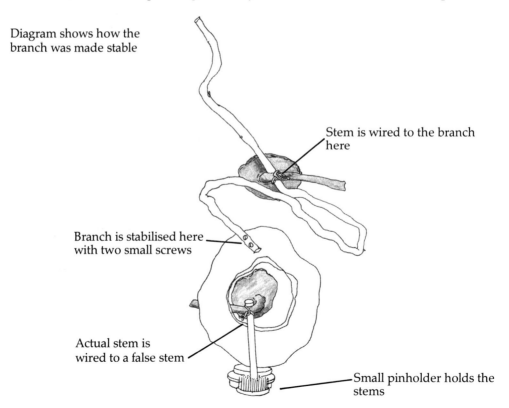

Stem is wired to the branch here

Branch is stabilised here with two small screws

Actual stem is wired to a false stem

Small pinholder holds the stems

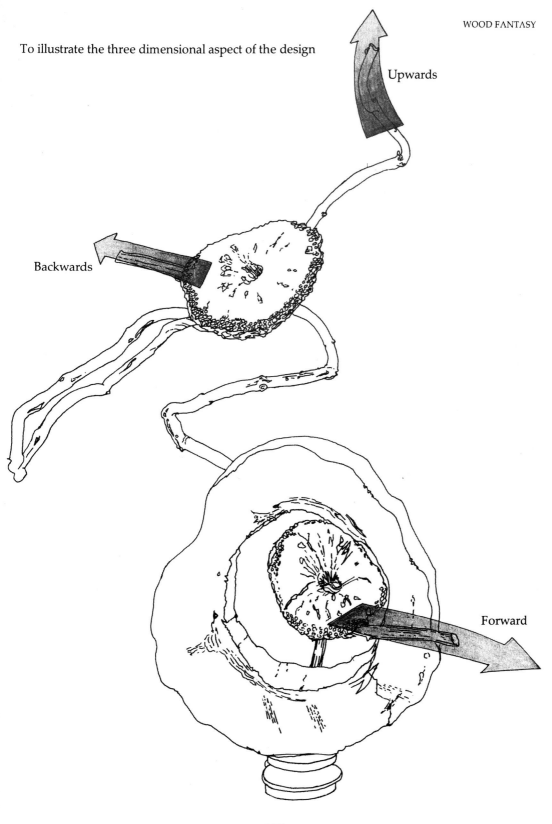

To illustrate the three dimensional aspect of the design

Upwards

Backwards

Forward

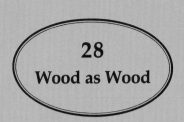

28
Wood as Wood

In the previous composition the wood functioned solely as an element of design, and there was no attempt at naturalistic effects of presentation.

Its major design assets are still highlighted in this instance also, but the placement and selection of plant material added relates more to the natural than before.

A couple of wooden bases replace the sophisticated staging to create a more rustic atmosphere. These also give the design a more conventional balance and a different line of movement.

The sparkling colour of the fresh flower and leaves, combined with a branch of vigorous movement, conveys the pattern of growth, and the garden. In association with the wood, there is an impression of new and dormant plants existing naturally together.

The branch, which replaces the dried one of the previous arrangement is Corylus contorta (contorted hazel) stripped of its leaves, which in summer hides the beauty of its distinctive line, and is not particularly attractive.

So.here too, the natural is to a degree subordinated to the design requirements, and the initial selection influenced by the particular effects required in presentation. The flower for instance defines the shape of the wood and harmonises in scale with the void. The branch gives animation to rhythm, and extra emphasis to the line of the wood and this is more effective with the slight alteration in natural appearance.

Basically, the intent is to present naturalistically but without reducing design impact.

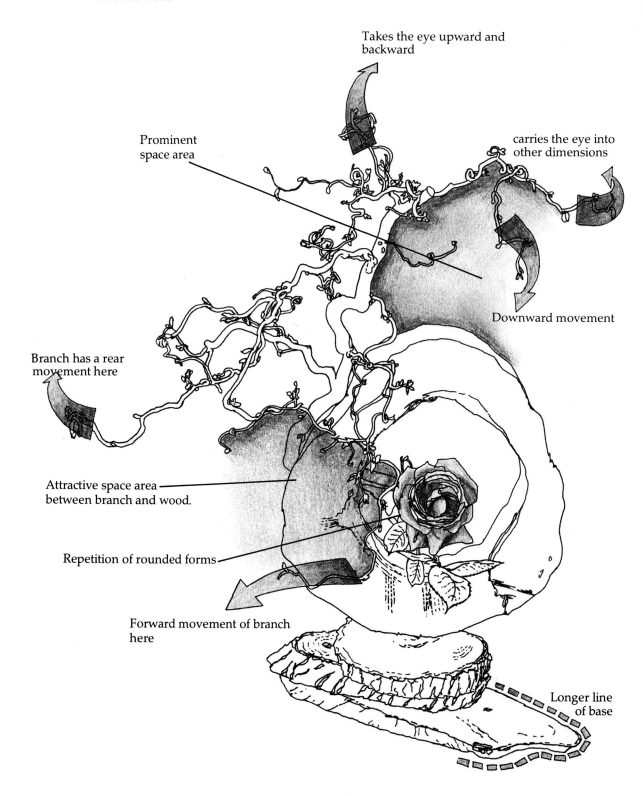

Takes the eye upward and backward

carries the eye into other dimensions

Prominent space area

Downward movement

Branch has a rear movement here

Attractive space area between branch and wood.

Repetition of rounded forms

Forward movement of branch here

Longer line of base

Design Analysis

As in the previous design, form and space are strongly contrasted, with one enhancing the effect of the other.

Space is well defined around the form of the rose, and spaces in the pattern of the branch.

Space beneath the wood and the bases also enhances presentation. The vigorous line of the branch repeating the outline of the wood, enlivens the rhythm of the design. The placement of the three separate bases also adds a rhythmic line.

Advancing and receding colours also add movement, whereas in the previous design, the bases were organised to give the wood a more precarious balance and the design a space orientated aspect. The bases here give the arrangement a more formal balance. The extra length of the lower base on the right balances the greater dimension of the branch to the left, but this does not over-compensate the effect, and overall balance is kept interesting and dynamic through the distribution of space and solid.

Textures are mainly matt and smooth, with the roughness in the pattern of the twigs and edges of the bases as contrast.

The colour contrast is pleasing, but not over-dramatised, so as to preserve the sculptural emphasis and rhythmic aspect of the design.

The branch is actually three-dimensional and has considerable vitality.

Study the diagram for the different lines of movement and notice the relationship of space and solid throughout.

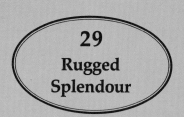

29
Rugged Splendour

Nature has excelled herself in this remarkable piece of sculpture. No wood carver anywhere could surely improve upon this. The major piece is very striking, and is complemented by a lesser sized, but also, interesting structure. The two combined with smooth brown pebbles and elegant flowers, unite to make a composition of beautiful objects that is visually satisfying.

So the design can be appreciated just for its sculptural line, interest of texture, or rich colour harmony, and the way the units are organised to display their major features for decorative effect.

But the shape and structure of wood can also evoke images that appeal to the imagination and inspire interpretations. The line of the wood here, for instance, as well as giving the design its major impact, is also powerfully expressive, and invites contemplation and comment. To some, it might suggest a bird in flight, to others perhaps a mysterious shape in space. It reminded my younger son of an angel's wing poised in graceful motion. My husband also favoured the sense of movement the line of the wood conveyed – but his image was of a more stirring and vigorous nature, visualised in, and I quote, 'A winged messenger from the Gods circling the earth'. Which proves how strongly personal response is in colouring impressions and interpretation.

Your own reaction might again be totally different and the character or outline of the wood might evoke the contours of rocks or rugged hills, or a valley of deep shadows. Or the combination of the two shapes may suggest the silhouette of immense and brooding figures on the landscape, reminiscent of certain Henry Moore sculptures in the open. A fertile imagination will weave its own fantasy to give whatever image is presented its unique interpretation.

Design Analysis

The most expressive line is at the top of the wood, which carries rhythm in a strong horizontal line, supported by the pattern of the background. The secondary movements of the wood and diagonal line of the flowers add contrast and further vitality. The lower leaves and larger pebbles supply forward movement – background draws the eye to a larger distance.

The spaces defined by the irregular forms are also dynamic, and influence rhythm, increase the depth illusion, and add to the beauty of the design.

Space beneath the bases supporting the major wood, and around each item in the foreground, and placements at different levels also improve rhythm, and enhance presentation.

Textures of the wood are predominantly smooth with repetition in stones and flowers. The contrast of a rougher texture is supplied by the dried hellebore leaves and background effects. Bases are matt and dull.

Colour harmony is crisp with the sharper contrast of the leaves and flowers accentuating the subtler variation of the lighter and darker values of brown in the other subjects.

The sombre shadowy tones of the background increases atmosphere and expressiveness of the interpretation.

Solid and space distribution controls the balance, with the powerful line of the wood and of the flowers together with the dramatic space area on the top left, countered by the eye-catching space, and rounded contours of the wood and large space area on the right.

Technique

No great problem with assembling. The larger wood is self-supporting like the smaller, a well pinholder is tucked unobtrusively between the two.

Two bases lift the major sculpture off the ground. The background is studio paper painted with powder paints.

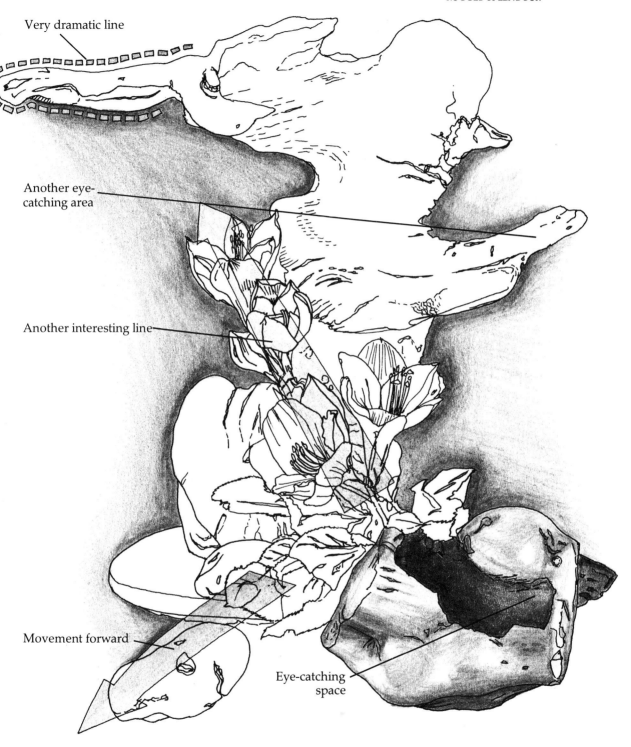

Very dramatic line

Another eye-catching area

Another interesting line

Movement forward

Eye-catching space

In black and white the dramatic line of the wood is strongly emphasised

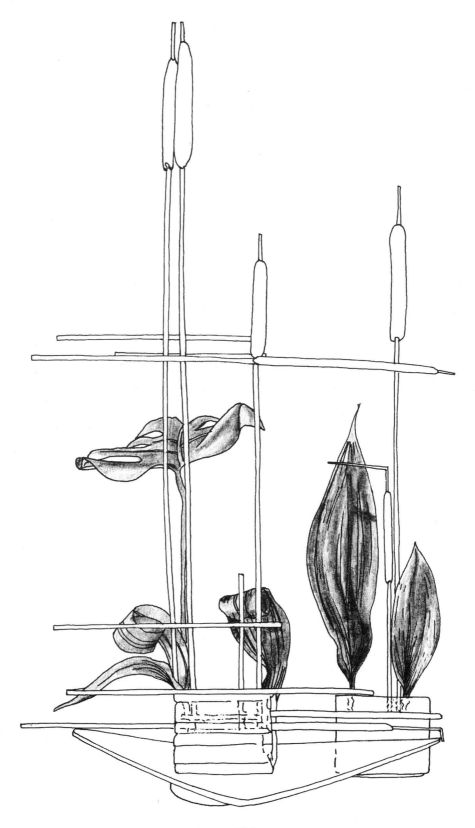

126

Introducing Abstract – Its Philosophy and Principles

An arrangement in the abstract style is based on the theories of abstract art, with plant material as medium. Basically, it is a style with little if any naturalistic aspects, for the aim is not to emulate nature or to imitate natural appearance but to capture the essence of the inherent characteristics of a subject. A quality or aspect of this is subtracted by the mind and presented according to the personal impression.

It is not superior to the traditional arrangement or representational style, and not all plant material is entirely suitable or practical. But it is another area of exploration, where the designer is free to experiment with the medium to discover deeper aspects, and to be inventive and original.

Every trend in Art is open to speculation and to criticism. Many question the ethics of tampering with natural effects, maintaining that Nature has already established colour, texture, shape and pattern of the plant material, and that this is varied and abundant enough already. Why then, it is asked, this need and inclination to alter or to re-arrange the system?

Advocates of abstract art on the other hand, would argue that the purity of form, and inherent character of a subject is enhanced, and given greater significance, when distracting or superfluous detail is removed to leave the simple basic shape or essential underlying structure.

Both points of view are valid and worthy of consideration. The traditional style and the naturalistic arrangement is the most effective way of displaying the plant material's natural surface beauty but the deeper research and power of simplicity defend the aims of the abstract style. If so inclined, one can be involved with both, and benefit from their different artistic aspirations.

It would be true to say that the theories of abstraction are adopted daily when the eye selects the important from the unimportant in the world around us. Otherwise sight and sense would be in a state of constant confusion. A lawyer's document is the summary of the main points of the case – its highlights – for easier reference and assessment. Children's drawings of a figure, tree or animal are usually simplified to show the major characteristics only. The child concentrates on the basic shape of the objects, the pyramid of a tree, or the roundness of a human figure, the essential form rather than the detail.

Even in the most conventional flower arrangement there is a careful selection of the elements, when flowers are considered for their shape, advancing and receding colours, or symbols of emotion. The process however is more deliberate and consciously applied by the designer in abstract style, where there is a different approach and attitude.

Though there is a deliberate move away from the natural the arranger is still involved with nature and the visible world and is quite likely to become more observant of universal laws and natural phenomena in searching for new ideas for designing. The patterns, shapes and colours all around may be regarded with greater interest and curiosity, as the designer's eye considers the range of shapes in the circle, cone, pyramid, oval, or the free-form shapes of clouds, rocks and rugged hills. There are lines in nature that might stimulate ideas, like a vertical row of poplars, the low line where earth meets sky, and furrowed fields, zig-zag of lightning, spiral of smoke, and the beautiful symmetry in the radiating petals of a daisy.

Or there is inspiration from the rhythms of nature in the play of light and shadow, sun and cloud, night and day – in the dance of the leaves, and falling rain.

Even on a more prosaic level there are many sources of stimulus to a keen designer in the prolific patterns and galaxy of objects in the workaday world, like beautiful patterns in machinery, the skyline of a city, stone walls and grids and wooden gates, or a jumble of houses on a hillside. Similarly inspiration for textural emphasis of a design may come from old rope and rust and weathered brick, or the sophisticated shine of plastic, and gleam of metal. The man-made shapes we see everyday can prompt an abstract pattern. Modern architecture at its best has great simplicity and lack of ornamentation and what could be more inspiring as shape and line than that miraculous piece of modern technology the Concorde, which is the very essence and epitome of graceful speed.

Even the more vulgar additions of the modern age, telegraph poles in their solid symmetry, television aerials, multi-storey car parks, and the rich confusion of advertising symbols, speak the language of design in one way or another. Looking at the world with a probing eye for fresh discoveries is an absorbing occupation, and for the designer an extremely productive one as well.

Design Characteristics

Abstraction in art can imply two things. The first is that there is no reference to any subject, and the painting, drawing or sculpture is purely a composition of shapes, space, and areas of colour and texture. No theme is portrayed or feeling expressed and the major interest is the design itself.

Applied to the art of flower arrangement it establishes the principle in:
1. Striking pattern
2. Methodical arrangement, and careful balance of line, form, texture, and colour to create order and harmony and visual appeal
3. Lack of ornamentation and surface detail
4. Dynamic use of space.

In the second the content is more lyrical, and an idealised, or simplified form of something derived from the observed, external world which can be coloured by emotion. In this instance, plants become symbols of expression, and the design is characterised by
1. A definite emotive quality
2. Symbolic use of the elements
3. A simplified or exaggerated presentation of the subject for a stronger statement.

In both instances there is
1. Non-naturalistic use and exploitation of the plant material
2. Unconventional placements
3. Elimination of detail
4. Simplified presentation
5. No fixed centre of interest – the units function independently without radiating from one central point
6. Space as a positive part of the rhythm, depth and balance – or expressive content
7. Lack of transitional effects
8. Strong contrasts
9. Strong silhouette.

Design Technique

Since naturalistic effects and actual representation are not of primary importance, and the aim is for greater emphasis of design quality or expressive content, the designer adopts various techniques to

promote these requirements:
1. With the plant material
2. With the method of assembling.

Through the medium

Its effectiveness for pattern or interpretation is often greater with a change from natural appearance. This can be achieved by:
1. A change of shape or line, for instance strap leaves or other pliable subjects like vines, can be looped or curved into geometric shapes. Broad leaves can be furled or folded. Single flowers closely bunched together to lose their natural outline to become points of emphasis of colour and texture.
2. Surface qualities exaggerated for added emphasis with an alien texture. Dried, preserved, or skeletonised subjects are to a degree altered texturally. Sand, grit, crushed shells or small seeds alters the natural surface even more.
3. Colour change, with paint, dye, bleach and other agents.

Enthusiasm however, should be tempered with discretion and the techniques adopted only if these bring the essential qualities featured more closely to notice – subtle changes are often more effective than crude effects.

Through the Organisation of the Units

Non-naturalistic effects become more pronounced when the units are organised in an unconventional way. The arranger does not work to a pre-determined pattern, but places the material wherever it benefits the design or interpretation.
1. The items can assume any position in the format of the composition
2. All the design principles can be exaggerated

3. Something less conventional than a vase is often used, like plinths, rods, wires or plastic or wooden structures. Plants may be impaled on these, or organised out of the container so they appear suspended in space
4. Backgrounds are often used to incorporate part of the design and to become integrated with the composition
5. The units may hang, or actually move, in space.

The more both techniques are exploited to the limits, the more abstract the design. Sometimes perhaps, the arranger moves slightly out of orbit, to embrace the concepts of other modern art forms with structures not unlike modern sculpture. But the greater majority of designs in this area are free-form compositions based on the principles of abstraction, with plant material as the designing symbols. Total abstraction rejects all recognisable objects and rational relationships – a difficult process with the flower arranger's medium. It may therefore be preferable to say 'in the abstract style', as this is a clearer indication of the intent of the design. This implication is of a style that adopts the philosophy and concepts of abstract art within the limits set by the medium, and adapted to its designing possibilities and major features. It is an area with different aims and aspirations to the representational or naturalistic style.

The examples that follow are based on these theories and the experiments illustrate the various techniques discussed, and how these are influenced and sometimes controlled by the nature of the plant material. Designs are evaluated in the context of how the principles apply, and are adapted to the art of flower arranging.

129

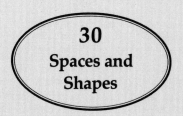

30
Spaces and Shapes

A design that is fairly easy to assemble and could be a useful example or gentle introduction to those embarking on the abstract style. Its theories are adapted to displaying plant material in a simple presentation that emphasises their individual qualities, and the example features several design tendencies typical of this style that are easy to explain to the less experienced.

Since the main constituents are fresh plants, the assembling technique is based on the need to have the stems in water, without the mechanics being too obvious and clumsy.

To enhance the presentation with a greater sense of depth, and to bring each leaf into greater focus, a slender rectangular structure made with thin reedmace was placed in the forefront to give the subjects placed behind greater definition.

One of the ambiguities of discussing abstract design as applied to flower arranging is that, whilst the plants are considered purely as elements of design, it is difficult to disregard completely their natural identity.

Here, for instance, whilst the leaves stand out as shapes, with different lines of direction which determine the pattern of the design, nevertheless one tends to think of their familiar associations as monstera and aspidistra plants, and especially so, when their natural appearances are maintained.

The aim however, is not to stress the naturalistic aspect, but to emphasise the abstract qualities of form and line that generate design force. Whilst outward beauty can still be appreciated, the arranger is more concerned in making us aware of the more essential, inherent, properties of the material. It could perhaps be said that there is a shift of emphasis, from the general to the personal, with the presentation coloured by the individual point of view rather than the more conventionally or universally accepted.

Drawing illustrates how each item is
clearly defined as shape and line

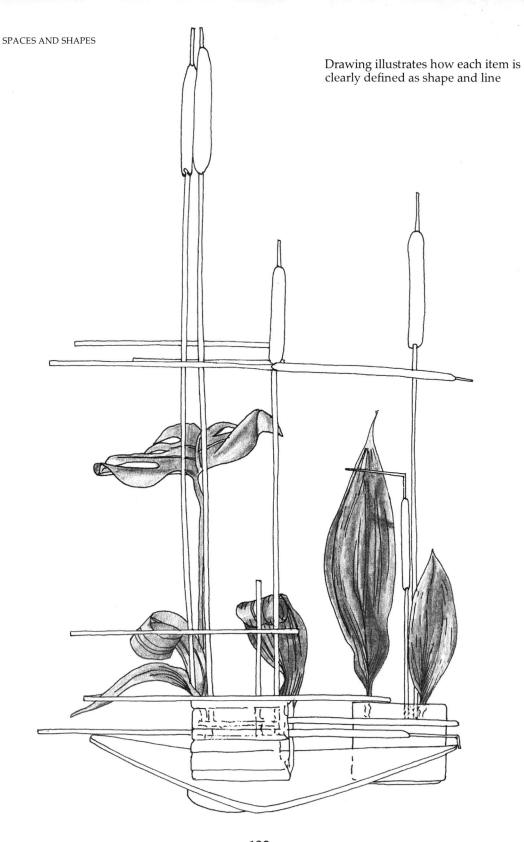

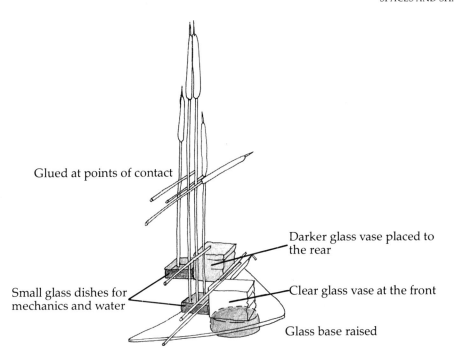

Glued at points of contact

Darker glass vase placed to the rear

Small glass dishes for mechanics and water

Clear glass vase at the front

Glass base raised

Design Analysis

Many of the design characteristics of an arrangement in the abstract style are featured in this example.

An unconventional assembling. Notice the organisation of each item; without the conventional radiation from one central area, each leaf has its distinctive placement, and functions in an individual way rather than as part of a conventional grouping.

Emphasis. Each group is an area of interest, but no unit is over-dominant and the eye is encouraged to inspect all aspects of the design with comparable appreciation.

Eliminating Detail. Though there is variety, there are no unnecessary additions to detract from the simplicity of the pattern. Everything used is necessary to the design structure and its unity. The two containers for example, though introduced for technical reasons, still play an important part in the line, form and textural interest of the design; the

base is also involved in the rhythm and pattern of the composition.

Balance. This is not conventionally organised, and each placement affects the overall balance.

The taller line created by the reedmace on the left, is balanced by the thicker sections on the right, and the darker glass container.

The visual weight of the two strong verticals created by the aspidistra leaves on the right, are countered by the largest leaf (monstera) on the left and the diagonal pull of the lower aspidistras.

Further Technical Details

The two Swedish glass vases, turned on their sides, hide two small glass dishes for pinholders and water.

A clear triangular glass base raised on a glass ash-tray, unites the two separate groups of material without being too obvious.

The reedmace were glued together at the points of contact.

133

31
Pattern on
Pattern

Another experiment with a certain type of plant material, to create an interesting pattern, not unlike the previous composition in concept and presentation. This time however the items are all dried plants, permitting greater opportunity for an original layout with more inventive effects.

Without the need to conform to conventional designing, the arranger can exploit the medium to suit the effect required. But its characteristic can still be the guide and inspiration. Many plants with striking features can add distinction to a very simple composition, once the designer is attuned to what they have to offer.

The nature of the plant material here for instance suggested the pattern most likely to suit their particular structure. The straight, smooth stems, devoid of detail, prompted a disciplined design with a pleasing structural clarity. The added bonus of distinctive texture and decorative pattern of the leaves adds further interest.

Their natural appearance is slightly altered, for apart from being dried, the palm fronds have been heavily trimmed for a sharper silhouette, and they are presented in a wholly unconventional fashion.

You might agree that the composition has a certain Mondrianesque quality in the right-angled relationships of vertical and horizontal lines. It has a comparable severity in its geometric pattern with certain Mondrian paintings, though primary colours do not feature here and focus is on line, space, and silhouette.

Clearly the very nature and characteristics of the medium exerts its influence and colours to a degree the final form of the composition.

Though not built around a subject, or the plant material consciously used for interpretation, it could be argued that the finished design has a certain expressiveness that could influence reaction, and might suggest a theme or subject. Do the very pointed forms suggest arrows, spears or other war-like objects to you? Primarily though it is the striking pattern that commands attention, through its rhythmic force and beauty of space and shape proportions.

Design Comments

The main designing aim here is to achieve a pattern that is pleasing in its clarity and sense of order, and at the same time has sufficient interest to hold attention.

Since there is very little plant material used, each unit must be carefully organised to suit the overall effect especially in the relationship of shape and space proportions.

The different rhythms operating here make an interesting study, for at first glance it might not be apparent there is much movement in the design, but the powerful vertical and horizontal lines compel the eye to move in their direction beyond the perimeters of the design.

In contrast the areas of space these lines define have the opposite value of inviting rest and contemplation. The enclosed area in the centre is the predominant pause area which stabilises the various active influences of the design. The space and solid elements and their organisation, also give the balance of the composition an interesting aspect, with a line here, a space there, adjusting each others visual weight. Notice how the longest spear at the bottom right hand and its extended horizontal line is balanced by the thicker line of the metal structure on the left and by the tallest vertical of the design.

Depth is generated also by the spaces in and beyond the physical boundaries of the composition. There are actually two separate placements here, with one placed forward from the other. The palm leaves at the base also have a forward movement to increase the sense of depth.

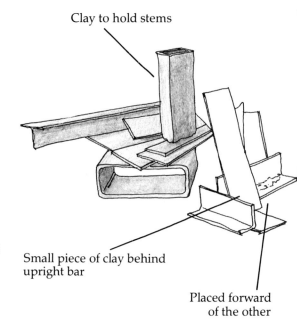

Clay to hold stems

Small piece of clay behind upright bar

Placed forward of the other

Technical Hints

This type of design needs to be immaculately put together, and this is really the only difficult aspect.

The vertical placements are easy, the horizontal more tricky, and the top two need very firm anchorage.

Can you use an electric drill? If not, hasten to learn, for it is a great asset. Modelling clay is useful for anchoring weighty and wayward stems – praise be to whoever invented both commodities.

The containers here are of welded iron with recesses to hold the clay for the vertical placements.

The crossing stems are held by tiny screws at the points of contact.

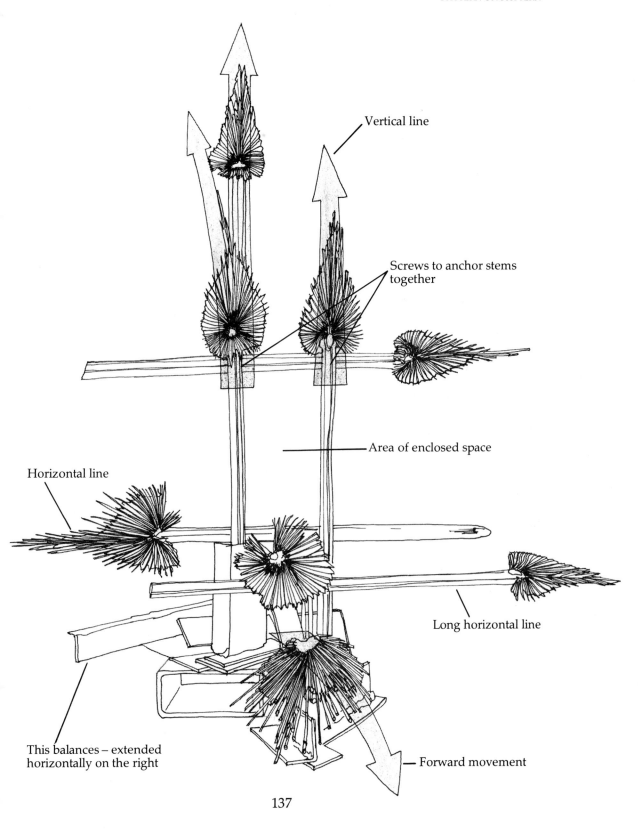

Vertical line

Screws to anchor stems together

Area of enclosed space

Horizontal line

Long horizontal line

This balances – extended horizontally on the right

Forward movement

137

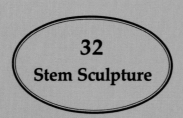

32

Stem Sculpture

This is not recommended as an exercise when you are impatient for results, for whilst it is not difficult to design, the constructing needs a steady hand and a reasonable amount of patience. This can be a useful design project, and an absorbing exercise once the pattern starts to evolve, and is a novel way of handling plant material. Though a casual decoration, the principles of balance, rhythm, contrast and variety are still involved and there is the satisfaction of using material that might otherwise end up on the compost heap, and costs nothing.

Many plants have hollow, woody stems, which perhaps are not particularly attractive or useful in their normal form, like the polyganum, *Rheum palmatum* and hogweed stalks used here. Divided into smaller sections, one is more aware of their pleasing roundness and clean line, texture and variation of colour, for in the altered form, the abstract qualities are more fully exploited, and easier to display.

There are several ways of assembling the units. If you like to work to a pre-determined pattern then a diagram to follow is the answer. This is probably the most fool-proof procedure, as it is easier to judge where size and shape belong in the balance of the design, and to plan the pattern. But those who operate like I do probably prefer to let things evolve, and make adjustments as the design develops, so as to enjoy the surprise at the finish. A compromise is to prepare the lay-out on a flat surface and work as though from a drawing, but remembering that some modifications might be necessary in the actual assembling to give depth and rhythm. Whichever method is adopted there is no set formula to stick to – no rules but those of good design. Whether you end up with a tree or teddy bear, a burst of bubbles or just a very pleasing shape.

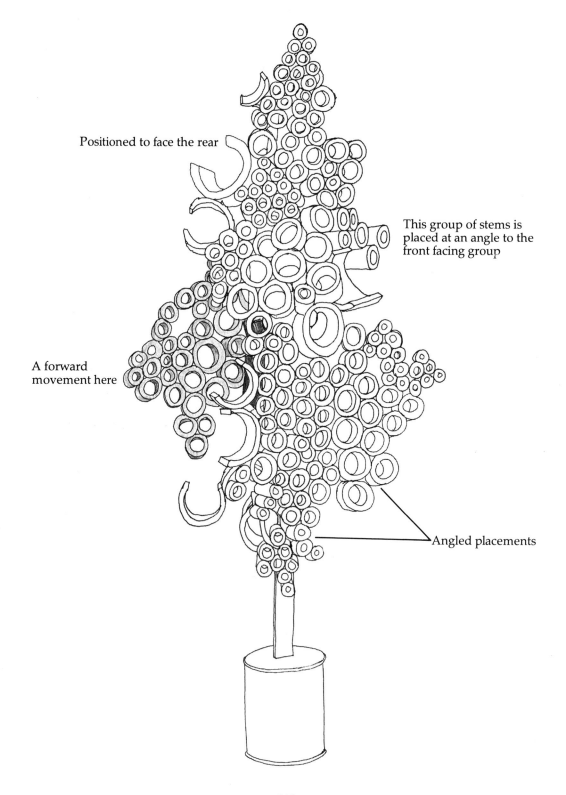

Positioned to face the rear

This group of stems is
placed at an angle to the
front facing group

A forward
movement here

Angled placements

140

Design Analysis

The structure is by no means a flat and two-dimensional structure, for the groups of stems are arranged at different angles for greater depth dimension.

These groups belong to two main sections, one placed at the back, the other to the front of the central support which also adds to the depth element.

Grouping the sizes of the circles creates a more orderly pattern, and gives the design added animation and rhythm.

The series of incomplete circles, strategically placed also helps to tie together through repetition the different units in a pleasing sequence.

The areas of space left here and there in the outline of the structure, and the variety of shape in the hollows, enhance the pattern and prevents too solid or monotonous an effect.

Colour contrasts are subtle and pleasing with the lighter hues giving the necessary definition and structural clarity. The brown of the background emphasises the monochromatic harmony. Different coloured backcloths would give other interesting effects to the spaces of the structure that could make stimulating comparisons. The natural colours of plants are usually very satisfying, and there is often a variety of hues in a single specimen, but experiments with added colour might well produce some exciting results.

How to assemble

Since the structure is raised, a strong support is the first essential. This is a ¼in thick slat of wood with another wider piece screwed on about a third of the way up for extra anchorage. This is inserted into a round jar filled with cement, coloured with acrylic paint to blend with the plant material. A few thin screws were driven in halfway along the front slat for extra support to the larger rings.

Work started at the centre, on the wider support, and progressed outwards. Front and back sections are glued at certain points of contact for added stability. A strong glue with good bonding was used. 'Superglue' is fantastic but dangerous, as without extreme caution, fingers stay glued together!

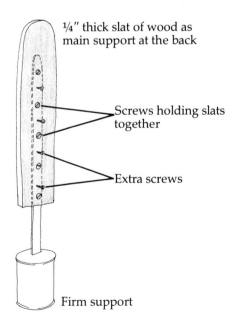

¼" thick slat of wood as main support at the back

Screws holding slats together

Extra screws

Firm support

141

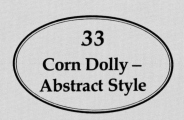

33
Corn Dolly –
Abstract Style

Straight stems are used here to make a delicate structure that has affinity with modern sculpture. It is another example where ordinary plants are used in an imaginative manner to highlight their special qualities, not always as apparent when massed together in the more conventional manner.

The stems of corn have for a long time been widely used in the making of corn dollies and other decorative motifs. Here they function purely in a design capacity. The design was not meant to represent anything in particular but planned as an interesting sculpture of natural plant material. The line, rhythm and nature of the design may suggest a subject to you or an aspect derived from it and you are quite free to form a personal judgement.

Is is amazing how lovely so many stems become when the outer husk is peeled away. Beautiful textures are often revealed, like the satiny, pearl-like sheen of straw, which is also an attractive colour. An appreciation of these qualities is expressed here in the design presentation and emphasis.

There are many other stems that could be used in similar ways. Roadside reeds are particularly adaptable, and many wayside, and cultivated grasses have attractive structures. These, like the corn and other cereals have the advantage of being extremely light in weight and easy to manipulate and to adapt to an interesting pattern. This flexibility makes it easier to create space and depth, and to control the rhythm of the design. So that although the units are visually light, a composition with considerable impact can still be achieved.

It might give you ideas for the winter months, when many of us try to sort out the mountainous collection of trivia collected in the year gone by. But do re-examine anything destined for the bonfire in case it has some further possibility – seedheads that have disintegrated, grasses past their glory, bullrushes that have 'blown', may have interesting stems still intact. These could all become the basis of your next design.

Design Comments

Placements are carefully organised to create as much interest as possible so as not to end up with a monotonous pattern that the eye soon tires of. A variety of movement into different planes counters this and adds a third dimension. There are lines which direct attention vertically, diagonally, forward, backward, and beyond the actual dimensions of the structure (see diagram). It is wise to plan the basic framework with these and other design requirements in mind. The support used here gives great flexibility to work in different planes. By using several stems glued together, it was possible to give greater definition to each line of movement, and depth illusion. The varied angle of each group also creates a pleasing pattern of light and shadow, which again enhances depth and rhythm. Another important factor is the compatibility of the framework to the material of the sculpture. Ideally, the support should be an integral part of the design and harmonise to this in colour, shape and texture. This unity again permits the pattern to be more open, with the structural stems adding to design interest rather than functioning just as a holding device (see diagram).

The 'explosion' at the top balances the solidity of the base, and maintains interest, and a lively rhythm high in the design.

Thinner stem fits into the _____ one below

Second vertical stem glued _____ to the other

Small angled stem fits into _____ the one below

Smaller sections jutting out _____

Three stems glued to the base and each other to form _____ the main support

Wooden cube _____

How the support was constructed

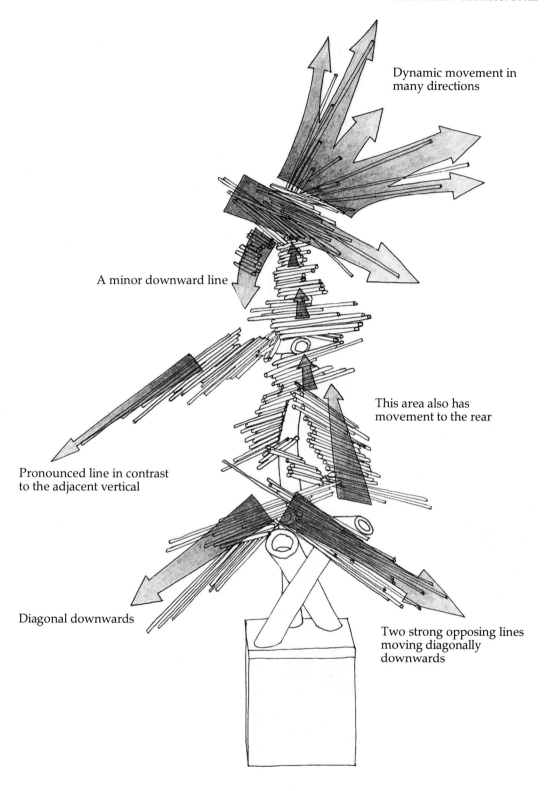

Dynamic movement in
many directions

A minor downward line

This area also has
movement to the rear

Pronounced line in contrast
to the adjacent vertical

Diagonal downwards

Two strong opposing lines
moving diagonally
downwards

145

34

**Grown on
the Moon**

This is rather a strange looking arrangement, and certainly not pretty,
judged by popular standards and ideas of beauty. But odd objects of
distinction appeal to the designer with a natural curiosity and liking for
the unusual. Some arrangements, though not conventionally beautiful,
are interesting or intriguing, different and imaginative, or a cause for
speculation.

Such compositions often do not qualify as *flower* arrangements, and can
be more aptly called sculptural compositions, where other forms of
plant life with interesting qualities are featured in an original way.
There are so many attractive forms of plant material quite apart from
flowers, that have their use as designing elements.

The initial inspiration for this natural structure was the bleached and
sanded wood, which came from Pretoria in South Africa. It has a
striking texture, colour and structural formation. There are two separate
pieces, one now attached to the other for a more impressive effect.
The fungi added for compatibility of colour and texture came from Italy,
and are also rather special with a similar, weathered sun-bleached
aspect that emphasises that of wood. Together they imply a strange,
lunar landscape, and the ruggedness of their outline is accentuated by
the loops of honeysuckle vine which repeat their line and pattern.

Nature's trivia with attractive or even peculiar features can give a
special atmosphere or aura to a design. The charm of such objects does
not rely on surface prettiness, but a quality that stirs the imagination.
This the arranger who likes the challenge of something different, can
use effectively for an original interpretation.

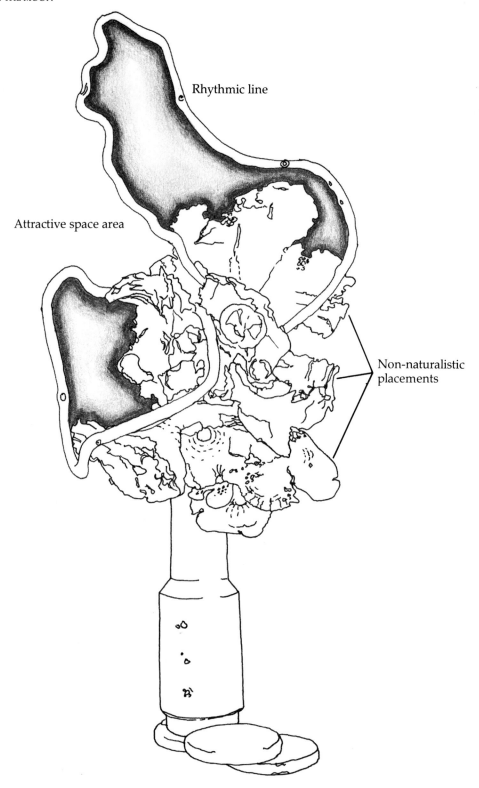

Rhythmic line

Attractive space area

Non-naturalistic
placements

Assembling Details

It was quite a difficult composition of varied aspects to put together.

First step was to stabilise the first piece of wood. This was drilled underneath to take a firm support, which was pushed into the container filled with sand.

Step two: second piece of wood was similarly anchored with a thin support from a hole drilled in the top piece driven into the lower.

Small holes were also drilled into the thicker end of the fungi to hold a cocktail stick.

A small lump of potter's clay placed on the bottom wood at the back holds the top two fungi and the ivy loops.

Container is a bleach bottle with the upper section cut off. The surface was coated with a wash of thinned down Polyfilla for a roughened surface, then coloured with art powder paints. The small bases are made of unfired clay.

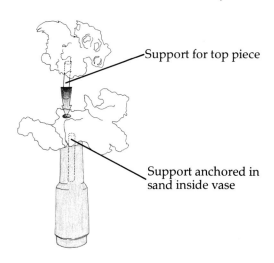

Support for top piece

Support anchored in sand inside vase

Design Observation

All the units are placed in an unnatural manner, and function merely as design elements. The fungi, for instance, are usually placed low, at the base of a naturalistic arrangement in keeping with growing habit. Here it is a positive, working part of the outline and structure of the design.

The wood has also lost its natural identity, and features just as a powerful line, shape and texture.

The vine encloses space and serves merely to accentuate the contours of the other items – and so gives greater design definition.

The placement of each unit also aids the design itself in:

Line – where items are grouped for continuity of movement. Repetition of line strengthens rhythm. The circular form of the container and round bases also make a rhythmic contribution.

Space – The whole design benefits from being raised in space. The loops of vine are placed where they give maximum depth through spatial definition.

Texture – Rough and smooth textures are organised to advance and recede. The wood has both smooth and rough textures, but is predominantly coarse. Fungi are matt and rough. The vine stripped of the outer husk is satiny and a contrasting texture. Container is rough, bases are smooth and matt.

Colour – Since this is monochromatic, a contrasting colour used as background highlights the subtle variation of hue in the constituents – and gives added value to the spaces of the design.

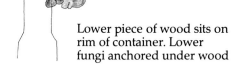

Lower piece of wood sits on rim of container. Lower fungi anchored under wood

Small stick in drilled hole

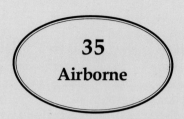

35
Airborne

This interpretation is again in complete contrast to the naturalistic or representational style, where the intention is to recreate scenes from nature as faithfully as possible. In abstract style, where there is no attempt to be literal or to present things as they appear to the eye, interpretations are a personal reflection, derived from the mind and the imagination.

Since the subject is not naturalistically portrayed, it can be presented in an idealised, or simplified form, or an aspect or quality derived from it, emphasised or exaggerated for greater interpretation.

This procedure gives the designer considerable opportunity to be original and imaginative. It does not mean that it is easier than the representational style, where natural laws are a guide and outward appearance help to prompt the interpretation to the viewer. As already mentioned, the artist in abstract style has to rely more on design impact and symbolic strength of the plant material and has to maximise its effectiveness as an element of design. Form, colour, texture and general character is therefore often altered to strengthen its potential. For the same reason, the units are not organised conventionally, but placed wherever they perform the greatest service to the pattern and expression of the design.

Since there is only one type of plant material used here, its surface colour and texture has been altered and its predominant features exaggerated for greater emphasis.

Again, the method of assembling is not naturalistic, with each unit in a placement which contributes to the theme implied.

Both these procedures are naturally easier and more practical with certain types of plant material. With subjects that are already dried and normal appearances already altered, one feels less inhibited in changing colour and texture, and it is easier to arrange these in unconventional positions since the stems need not be in water.

Design Comments

A buoyant movement, essential to the interpretation, is maintained throughout the design through placements organised to 'move' in different directions.

The topmost group has a strong descending line – sharply contrasted by the horizontal direction in the foreground.

The various diagonal lines also sustain the rhythm.

Space and depth are created by the varied placements, and the transparent acrylic enhances these features.

The plant material is a cultivated thorn with the impressive name of *Colletia infasta (Cruciata)*. It has been dried and then sprayed with silver paint touched up here and there with a hint of pink-red. It is very decorative in structure, like winged insects or small planes making a dive downwards through the air.

Design Technique

The theme suggests movement in space and to carry out the illusion it was necessary to organise the units to appear suspended without too obvious a support.

Strips of clear acrylic, visually light and unobtrusive seemed a good idea. The longest strips were anchored in a tall glass bottle. This enabled me to glue on several smaller pieces at different levels to give a variety of possible placements.

For extra safety the plants could be glued to the supports (with a special acrylic adhesive).

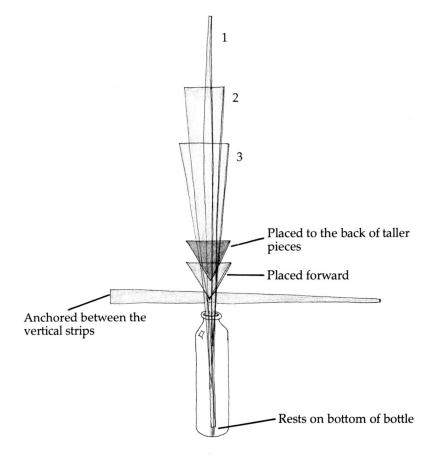

1

2

3

Placed to the back of taller pieces

Placed forward

Anchored between the vertical strips

Rests on bottom of bottle

Diagram showing the various lines of the design

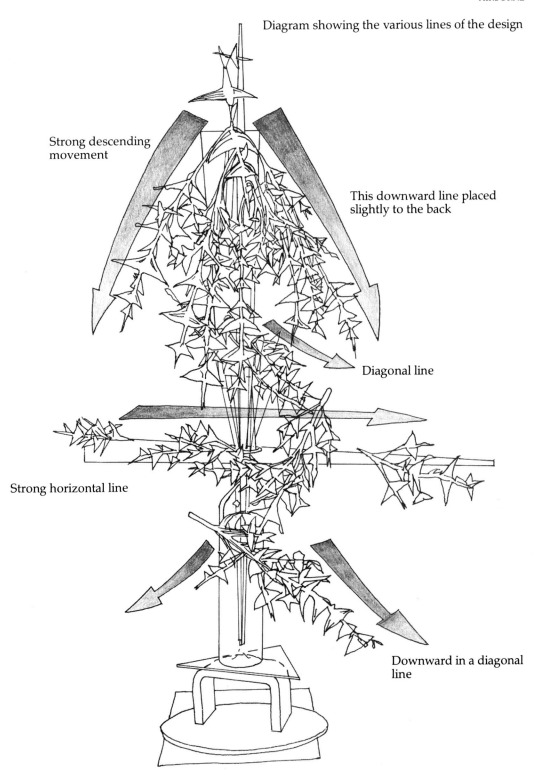

Strong descending
movement

This downward line placed
slightly to the back

Diagonal line

Strong horizontal line

Downward in a diagonal
line

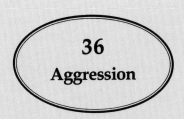

36
Aggression

The expression of strong emotion is the basic theme of this abstract design. It interprets a mood or feeling which could be anger, hatred, violence or revenge. These are not pleasant emotions, and the arrangement is not a 'pretty' one, though it does not necessarily reflect the mood I was in at the time!

A look at some of the well known expressionist paintings reveals the intensity of feeling expressed. This is often achieved with vivid, shocking colour combinations, or exaggerated lines and distorted images. Clearly the expression of emotion is more important than the conventional likeness of the subject matter.

As the painter with palette, the flower arranger attempts an expression through the nature and character of the plant material selecting the line, form, colour and texture most likely to generate the mood and convey the atmosphere of the theme. By considering the inherent qualities of the plants, their unique expressiveness can be the symbols for interpretation.

The thorns used in the arrangement here evoke different responses to those of the previous example. The line is more aggressive and disturbing, and coloured black, the feeling is intensified. The sharp angles of the blackened palms strengthens the symbolism.

You might not care to live with this kind of arrangement, with its harsh, strident colours, and tortuous lines. It is not meant to soothe or pacify and is more of an exhibition piece or an illustrative  exercise for the class-room. It might even be of therapeutic value, as a release from pent-up feelings or repressed anger. So, next time you are in a rage, let it bubble out into a brilliant interpretation.

Design Assessment

All the materials here work for the dominant atmosphere of the design. Pointed jagged forms and irregular lines that create a sharp, staccato rhythm suggest unrest or turmoil.

Textures are harsh and abrasive with natural surface qualities altered for extra emphasis.

Colours are strong and sharply contrasting. The strongest hue – high in the design adds drama, with the red symbolic of strong emotion.

Placements are non-naturalistic to promote the design force of the material. The expressiveness of line and form is intensified and the rhythm of the design made more powerful by these placements.

Container and plant material integrate and unite in design purpose, and whilst placements are unconventional, the line, form, space and colour distribution work for overall balance.

The arrangement was photographed against two different backgrounds for comparison of the two effects. The lighter grey sharpens the detail and throws everything into greater relief, whilst the darker grey tends to soften outlines for a more subtle and speculative atmosphere.

Technique of Construction

Achieving a stable frame-work is the most difficult aspect.

First Requirement – A strong, steady prop that looks part of the design.

First Step – Two fairly flat pieces of wood have thin supports glued at the back (those ice lolly sticks again). Wood painted matt black.

Second Step – Metal container half filled with sand for stability. A few inches of modelling clay on top of this anchors the wood, one in front of the other, small gap left between.

To Assemble – Palms are held together between the slats by a thin wire. Thorn; one piece rests on wood at the top. The second piece is anchored to the other at the top. The lower end rests on container. Flowers, in small glass tubes fixed with wire between the gap in the wood.

A lot of work? Yes, but the effort, is very character building!

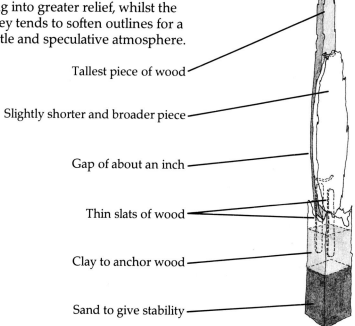

Tallest piece of wood

Slightly shorter and broader piece

Gap of about an inch

Thin slats of wood

Clay to anchor wood

Sand to give stability

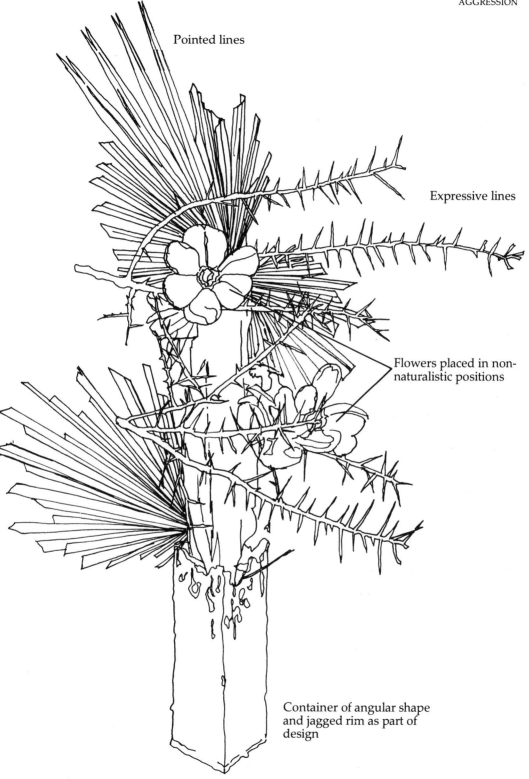

Pointed lines

Expressive lines

Flowers placed in non-
naturalistic positions

Container of angular shape
and jagged rim as part of
design

157

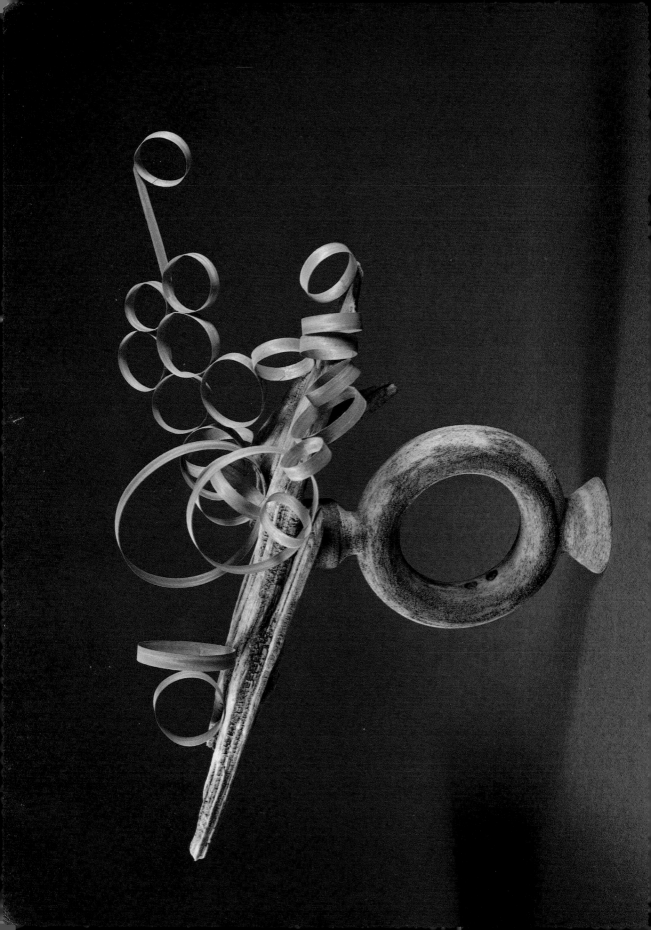

37
Salute to Speed

The line of this sculptural composition has considerable impact, and the design pattern is very arresting. It illustrates again how a few well-chosen subjects can be used to form the basis of a visually satisfying design.

This abstract style arrangement again uses plant material in an expressive capacity and not merely for design pattern, with the plants as symbols of expression for the interpretation.

The initial motivation came from the piece of driftwood, which now forms the pivot of the design structure, and governs the character and expressiveness of the composition. Driftwood has natural connotations which are not exploited here. In this example qualities other than its most obvious are used for design purposes. Its emotive line is symbolic of speed and movement – a quality intensified through its placement. Precariously poised on the edge of the container, it becomes a powerful diagonal line with exaggerated movement.

The expressiveness of this major element is given further emphasis by the supporting items, all of which contribute to design interest and interpretation. There is nothing here that is not essential to these requirements. Even the container plays its part in the format of the composition and its expressiveness. In eliminating distracting detail and simplifying to leave an essential basic form, the message is communicated in a simple and direct way. It is clear from this and preceding examples, that the arranger in abstract style, without the help of recognisable accessories to tell the story, relies entirely on the expressiveness of the plant material and its organisation to give effective interpretation.

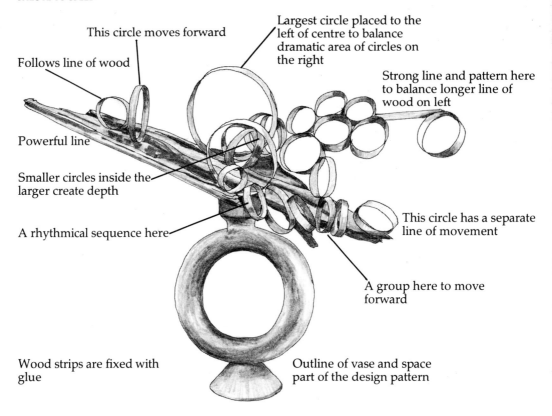

This circle moves forward

Largest circle placed to the left of centre to balance dramatic area of circles on the right

Follows line of wood

Strong line and pattern here to balance longer line of wood on left

Powerful line

Smaller circles inside the larger create depth

This circle has a separate line of movement

A rhythmical sequence here

A group here to move forward

Wood strips are fixed with glue

Outline of vase and space part of the design pattern

Design Observation

As already observed all the units are used as elements of design, and placed where they give maximum value to the expressive content. The wood presents an arresting shape and powerful line, to form the basic structure and expressiveness of the design.

This role is strengthened by the line of the circles made from strips of wood veneer which animates rhythm, and carries the eye into wider dimensions, and strengthens interpretation. Space is introduced by the second unit, both in the actual structure of the circles and extra sense of depth created by their line of movement.

The container again plays a prominent part in the space and rhythm.

The texture of the wood is interesting and eye-catching, with a variety of surface qualities. The rougher aspect is repeated in the texture of the container, the smoother matches that of the wood strips.

The colour element though not a prominent feature does contribute, along with textural contrasts, a subtle light and shade effect with advancing and receding areas. The darker background adds more definition to the enclosed spaces and sharpens the outline of the design.

Balance and Emphasis

A precarious quality is necessary to interpret the theme, yet the design must appear balanced. The intricate pattern on the right assures visual harmony by counter balancing the exaggerated line on the left.

Without the conventional central dominance, design interest is dispersed over several areas of emphasis. These are rhythmically united, but are physically separated as groups.